HAROLD LANG

1920/1985

IF HE ASKED ME,
I COULD WRITE A BOOK

DANNI BAYLES-YEAGER

Note for Librarians: A cataloguing record for this book is available from Library and Archives Canada at www.collectionscanada.ca/amicus/index-e.html

ISBN 1-4120-7135-6

Printed in Victoria, BC, Canada. Printed on paper with minimum 30% recycled fibre. Trafford's print shop runs on "green energy" from solar, wind and other environmentally-friendly power sources.

Offices in Canada, USA, Ireland and UK

This book was published *on-demand* in cooperation with Trafford Publishing. On-demand publishing is a unique process and service of making a book available for retail sale to the public taking advantage of on-demand manufacturing and Internet marketing. On-demand publishing includes promotions, retail sales, manufacturing, order fulfilment, accounting and collecting royalties on behalf of the author.

Book sales for North America and international:
Trafford Publishing, 6E–2333 Government St.,
Victoria, BC V8T 4P4 CANADA
phone 250 383 6864 (toll-free 1 888 232 4444)
fax 250 383 6804; email to orders@trafford.com

Book sales in Europe:
Trafford Publishing (UK) Limited, 9 Park End Street, 2nd Floor
Oxford, UK OX1 1HH UNITED KINGDOM
phone 44 (0)1865 722 113 (local rate 0845 230 9601)
facsimile 44 (0)1865 722 868; info.uk@trafford.com

Order online at:
trafford.com/05-2030

10 9 8 7 6 5 4 3 2

Acknowledgments

<u>*to all those who helped me complete this labor of love:*</u>

Kaye Ballard - Harold's buddy and now my "neighbor." It's been such fun talking to you.

Carol Bruce - Harold's "Pal Joey" co-star on the road and in London, for her gracious interview.

Helen Gallagher – a great star and Harold's long-time dancing partner. I enjoyed our telephone conversations so much. You reminded me why it was impossible not to love this man.

Alois Lang, Jr. - Harold's brother and a supporter of thes efforts. *(Sadly, Alois died in May 2002)*

Mike Madill - Thank you for the dance program at CSU-Chico. It was "the best of times."

Vicky Mahoney- for the hours of audiotape transcription.

PALM - the Performing Arts Library and Museum of San Francisco, for their preservation of the history of the San Francisco (Opera) Ballet.

Dave Peoples - Jefferson High School librarian (Daly City, CA) for his help in finding archival material on Harold's birthplace.

Thomas Steele - one of the friends who made it possible for Harold to die in his own home, and a tremendous help in the undertaking of this book.

Randy Wonzong, Phd - for candidly remembering the CSU-Chico Theatre Arts program.

<u>*And to Harold's many friends who shared their love and memories*</u>:

Nannette Fabray, Barbara Cook, Bibi Osterwald, Fredrick Tucker *(for the great Alice Pearce photo)*, and several others who asked to remain anonymous.

****

<u>*Special personal acknowledgments to:*</u>

Elva Rita Stone Bayles - for teaching me to read and to waltz.

Francis Arthur Bayles - for taking me to see my first musical, *Showboat*.

Gary Collier, Ph.d - for introducing me to Lord Peter Wimsey.

Donna Henry (Harter) - for making me take that fantastic high school drama class.

Carol Vikse - for teaching that fantastic high school drama class.

Phyllis Williams - Cecchetti Ballet Method *dominatrix par excellence,* who gave me a new life.

This book is dedicated to my husband,

Matt A. Yeager,

who not only put up with my many years of
unpaid writing efforts but also edited
and helped finance the project.

———————

Dearest, my undying gratitude.

Table of Contents

(Appendices listed on following page)

Appendices

Introduction

"Beware what you wish for. You might get it."
(Maybe that should have been the subtitle of this book.)

This is a story about a man who is largely forgotten today, even by those who still remember him. If that sounds paradoxical, so does the life of Harold Lang.

I reminded Harold of my promise to write his biography the night before heading to San Francisco in the summer of 1985 for a dance conference. My friend and mentor of the last fifteen years was dying of pancreatic cancer. His students were watching him shrink in front of their eyes and, like the Cheshire Cat, it eerily seemed like his grin would be the last thing to fade away. The night before the conference began I looked at him and decided not to go. But the Bay Area was Harold's old stomping grounds and he wouldn't hear of it. "Go, and bring me back all the gossip!" That was an order. I left at five the next morning.

I got home three days later to find a message from a friend that he had just passed away. If any of us cried, it was in relief that we wouldn't have to watch him suffer. The last few months had been tough on everybody, but Harold was proud and wouldn't allow any pity-parties. One day I came for a visit and found his possessions stacked up to give away because he was "moving to a new place." He'd chosen some books and records for me... "if I wanted them." So far I hadn't cried in front of him, but that was close.

I'd never gotten up the courage to ask him straight out if he thought he'd been conning us all along. We were kids from the sticks of Northern California with a chain-smoking, alcoholic ex-Broadway star for a ballet teacher; gracious and charming, but with a phony 'theatrical' kind of charm. Was he trying to con us out of our dancing shoes? We didn't care. I don't think there was single one of us who hadn't seen at least part of the truth and it didn't matter. That was the sad part. I don't think he knew.

How he did this inspire such devotion? He had stories about his career and his "buddies," names like Robbins and Fosse that we only knew from books; that was part of it. Then there was his legendary generosity; we were *always* welcome at Harold's place. When we were there we could talk of all the things we felt passionate about - theater and dance; all the things we couldn't bring up around the dinner table with our own families. Not many families in Red Bluff, Los Molinos or even in Chico talked like that.

And he didn't just talk, he listened. He took us seriously and gave encouragement. If he made it from Daly City, why couldn't we make it from Chico? He gave us validation, God bless him. How could we not have loved him?

Harold, it took me a long time to write this book.
I've done my best, but I didn't really do you justice.

Harold's memory was never reliable when it came to dates. For example, according to his story he shipped out with the Ballet Russe de Monte Carlo just before his 20th birthday in 1940. However, if he actually did join them as they were on their way to film *Gaite Parisienne* at the Warner studios (as he also stated) it must have been 1941, and the Ballet Russe programs don't begin to include Harold as a company member until the 1941-42 season. In one of our audiotaped interviews, Harold clearly remembers dancing *Mademoiselle Angot* with Ballet Russe, when actually it was premiered by Ballet Theatre on October 10, 1943. (His memory may have been influenced by the fact that Massine, who also worked with Ballet Russe, was the choreographer.)

In editing the passages included from these interviews I have deleted erroneous material, but nothing has been added. Any quotes attributed to Harold are accurate and retain the flavor of an evening's discussion in his Chico living room.

The year 2000 brought Harold Lang's name back into the public's consciousness with two successful books; the biography of Gore Vidal by Fred Kaplan and Arthur Laurents' autobiography, *Original Story*. Both men at different times in their lives had been in love with Harold, and their memories couldn't help but be tinged with the acid of rejected romance. I have no doubt that much of what they remembered was true. Don't we all have a few wild stories from our younger days? I only hope that the fact that Harold went on to become a teacher and mentor in his later years can be remembered as well.

I have to take issue with some of the statements made by Arthur Laurents . He wrote that Harold changed his name when he became a serious performer (untrue, as shown by Harold's birth certificate, school records, etc.), that he was ashamed of his half-Mexican heritage (Harold boasted of his Hispanic lineage even in program bios of the period) and that he'd had his nose fixed (true, but I wonder how many of his other theatre contemporaries did the same.) In many ways the bitchiness of Laurents' writing speaks for itself. It sounds like it came from a mean-spirited old man who couldn't wait for his friends to drop dead so he could write about them.

Gore Vidal's memories were more genial; Harold drank too much, was exciting but an intellectual lightweight and was unable to commit to a relationship. The author of the biography, Fred Kaplan, was gracious in his response to my requests for more information. He would check his materials, he said, but thought that there was little from the Vidal research work to add.

The memories of long-lost love can be painful, romantic, embarrassing, sublime, pathetic, or any combination of the above. Maybe this explains the contrasts in the two men's memories, Actually, the most frequently repeated description of Harold I remember hearing was "sweet." From his famous friends to the college kids who hung around him like besotted bees; Harold was always described as being *sweet*. I still think of him that way, too.

To Danni
Sincerely
Harold

Rex Cooper and Harold Lang

CHAPTER 1: 1920-40

THE EARLY YEARS

Location: an Eastern Star Hall dance; Daly City, CA (circa 1925)

- edited from audiotape interview with Harold Lang; January 18, 1981-

****

I was sitting very politely next to my mother. All of a sudden I jumped up and ran out between the couples and started to dance, all by myself!

My mother was so embarrassed!!

She ran out on the floor, grabbed me by the wrist and pulled me back. "Oh, please excuse him."

That was my first solo.

****

You're going to think I'm nuts, but when I was going to high school I didn't know what I wanted to do. I used to visit one of my buddies – his dad ran the greenhouse for one of the cemeteries. I used to walk through the cemeteries up to the greenhouse to see my buddy and his dad.

 One day I got chewed out by the secretary in the [principal's] office. She was saying, "You are just not _oriented_ to school!" I thought, "Well, I'm not _Oriental_." I couldn't figure out what that meant, and she hurt me because she just lashed out at me. I hope she's in some slave market now!

So I walked through the cemetery and sat on a gravestone. Like a silent prayer, I said, "God, I wish I had some kind of _direction_. I wish there was something I could do." I realized I was sitting in the middle of all these tombstones and I said, "Isn't there something that one of you wanted to do and couldn't finish? I'd like to finish it."

I looked, and I was sitting on the tombstone of a violinist that died at a very young age. I forget his name, but as I got into dance I wondered, "Where did this all come from?"

And I thought maybe it was that strange little thing that flashed through my mind; that I wanted to finish what someone else had started.

I've always had a facility with languages and it never bothered me, just falling into Russian with the Russian ballet, speaking French, picking up Estonian, and of course Spanish, from the family. Then I read that my -- I don't know how many "greats" go into it -- my "great-great-great" grandfather was very fluent in Russian and all the other languages I picked up so easily. So it may be in the genes. I don't usually believe in the occult, but I think there is an aura of that.

I went to the Bancroft Library[1] to look up some more of my ancestry and they had bills of lading from my great-great-great-grandfather. 'Alcalde'-- it's like 'mayor' -- he was the second mayor of San Francisco and founded the Presidio. I noticed that he signed everything with a gigantic rubric; he'd finish "Martinez" and that Z would go on for hours. It would just spiral, and I thought, "I'm going to do that with my signature." I tried it and thought, "Naw, forget it."

My father's parents came from Alsace-Lorraine. It was originally French and I guess they shortened it [their name] when they came to this country. I know very little about my grandparents on my father's side. His parents died and he was adopted by -- oh, maybe he had another name! -- by the Langs in St. Louis, he and his brother. That side of the family I know so little about. He was practically an albino -- silver hair when he was about 20, very pale blue eyes, a very handsome man. I was with Ballet Theatre and they called me while we were on tour and told me that he had died.[2] I don't know how old I was -- age is something I never think about. He and my mother met very late in life. I think she had me when she was about thirty-six.

I remember one story my mother told me, that she met my father somehow socially. Her mother had died and it was a huge Spanish family -- like about twelve kids -- and she was working as a secretary and supporting the whole family. So she virtually raised all of her brothers and sisters. She met my dad later when her brothers and sisters were able to work and maintain themselves. She said one day my dad gave her some little, tiny diamond earrings. She took the streetcar home and she wondered why

---

[1] *University of California, Berkeley*
[2] *Alois Lang, Sr. died in 1949. Harold had rejoined the company briefly on tour.*

everyone was staring at her because she didn't have the earrings on, and she realized she was grinning a wide grin.

[Daly City] used to be called "The Garden City By The Sea" because a lot of Italian families settled there on the slopes and raised vegetables and flowers; our house was the only one standing. When dad went to work he'd have to walk from the streetcar down a muddy path to the house. Now it's all overgrown, and has so many memories for me – of Saturday baths and drying out in front of the fireplace; my brother and I, and reading magazines or newspapers. It echoes with my growing up, and when you go in [now] it's just hollow. My mother used to cook for the entire Spanish side of the family and they would come on every holiday and just overflow into the garden, through the house, out the front porch, down the street. They still populate my life... not materially, but they're there as part of my brain, part of my emotions. Maybe even stronger.

****

Daly City, circa 1931

(photo courtesy Bernard C. Winn)

(left) Vista Grande School

Harold Lang, 5th Grade (1930)

(photos courtesy Bernard C. Winn)

Original entrance to Jefferson High School Gym

(A 1938 classmate, Leon Fletcher, wrote on the school's alumni website: "One of my off-beat memories of Jefferson High was of Harold Lang, '38, suffering frequent hackling as he practiced his strenuous ballet exercises during his P.E. classes. He went on to become a major theatrical star.")

The Lang house at 14 Alp Street

Harold's only real "home" until his mother's death in 1979.

Daly City, 2000

I took the short train ride from San Francisco to Daly City, California and watched the scenery change from the mega-urban Bay Area to the small-town landscape of Harold Lang's home town. It didn't seem to have changed much in the last 80 years. The hills above the modest Alp Street house where Harold and his older brother, Al (Alois, Jr.) were raised are as bare now as when the boys played there in the 1920's. Jefferson High School is new, though; all except the gym and its lawn, just as Harold remembered it:

I used to stretch on the lawn at the high school. I was on the track team, and for some reason I just loved to stretch. I had no training at all. I didn't know what dance was about. I'd do splits, then what was kind of like "academic" or really beginning gymnastics. I'd do front-overs and cartwheels. I just sort of "had" to do it. I don't know why.

....

I'd flown up to the San Francisco Bay Area looking for the kid that Harold never seemed to remember being. To hear him tell it, his life officially began the day he watched a class at the San Francisco School of Ballet and was "born again" as a dancer. But I was writing a biography and thought there had to be something of his childhood left in Daly City.

According to the few people who remembered him from that era, Harold was a normal kid who loved to play, but shied away from organized "boys activities." His good friend Bernard Winn remembered trying to get him interested in the Boy Scouts, but after a few meetings Harold was a no-show. Bernard, a devoted Scout himself, was disappointed. However, when he later jokingly suggested they attend the Roller Derby Harold gave a surprisingly enthusiastic "Yes!" That wouldn't surprise anyone who knew him as an adult. (Boy Scouts? I don't think so, but *Roller Derby*?! So much more in Harold's character.)

One of the few clues I had was a copy of his birth certificate, which gives his name as simply "Harold Lang," although his middle name was always known to be "Richard." The certificate goes on to state that at the time of his birth his father was 44 years old and his mother 39, and their residence was that house he always called "home", 14 Alp Street. The baby was "born alive at 4am", December 21, 1920, delivered by John C. Newton, MD. That date would be important, since Harold's estimate of his age varied greatly throughout his life.

On the birth certificate his father's occupation is listed as "clerk", although Alois, Sr., was actually a *maitre'd* of the prestigious University Club of San Francisco. His mother, Adele ("Della") Martinez, was "the daughter of a prominent California Mexican-American family," according to his later bios.

The memories that Harold and Al both had of their youth were happy but limited, and they were always a little vague about their father's place in them. Helen Gallagher remembers Alois, Sr. as "not being there" for Harold, but she seemed not completely sure if it was a physical or figurative absenteeism. The questions I never asked either Al or Harold bother me now. Was their dad an alcoholic? Was there friction in the family over Harold's ballet dancing and Al's music career? In that era there must have been. Even today how many fathers want their sons to go into the ballet and piano playing? Were the sons estranged from the father? Was that one of the reasons Harold would jump ship with San Francisco Opera Ballet and go on the road with Ballet Russe de Monte Carlo? I had to comfort myself with the thought that even if I'd asked, both Harold and Al would have found a charming way of not answering. Certainly, Harold had been never estranged from his brother (a pianist, composer and music teacher) or his beloved mother.

Throughout his career the three were always in touch, and for every show Mother and Al were treated with trips to New York to see Harold perform on Broadway.

By most latter-day accounts, Harold has been labeled "bisexual."[1] I think a more truthful way of putting it was that he was such a narcissist he wanted to have 100% of the population desiring him instead of limiting himself to half. Based on my long friendship with him, I would say that Harold's own sexual inclinations were primarily homosexual. Like most gay professional men of the time I'm assuming he'd feel obligated to have occasional close, even physical, relationships with members of the opposite sex that might verge on the romantic (and in at one case, with Helen Gallagher, came extremely close), but this was usually a concession to the homophobic times and possibly not relationships they might have chosen otherwise. On his own as an adult, Harold by all accounts had a rollickingly gay sex life with no obvious regrets.

I should also add that I never came right out and asked Harold himself. Why? At the time it seemed so obvious and irrelevant, and you just didn't ask your college professors about their sex lives. Not that Harold was shy about sex; he had too many good stories about the people he'd worked with over the years for that. It was only by interviewing one of his former New York roommates that I got a glimpse of the young, enthusiastic and gymnastic Harold, and wished I'd been a little more curious (and had more nerve) when I had the tape recorder running.

Growing up gay/bisexual in small-town America at this time, however, must have been hell. San Francisco was just across the bay and even then had a large homosexual community, but it might as well have been on the other side of the moon as far as Harold was concerned. How could he have known what went on in the seamier sides of the city when the only times he got there it was for family-oriented activities? His dad went by

---

[1]Among others, *Something for the Boys: Musical Theater and Gay Culture,* the Vidal biography, etc.

train into work everyday, but train fare was money spent only for special trips in those Depression-era days. If there were gay men in his home town, I'm sure that no one discussed it in front of children. How did you handle feelings that a Catholic upbringing assured led straight to damnation? Maybe you survived by dreaming of getting away someday and becoming *Somebody*.

But becoming a Somebody didn't seem likely for this teenager in the Jefferson High class of 1938. Short, effeminate, with terrible acne and a less-than-stellar academic record, Harold wasn't in the running for "Most Likely To Succeed." And after Jefferson High School... what were his options? A lackluster scholar at best, there was little incentive, let alone financial means, for Harold to attend college. He needed a job. Luckily he was small and fast; just the ticket for a future Western Union messenger boy. In no time he found himself in a uniform and sitting on a bench in San Francisco with a line of similar young men, all waiting eagerly for the next call that might provide a sizable tip:

My first job was Western Union Messenger in San Francisco. I was given something to deliver -- I didn't realize that you handed to somebody else who's out on a truck or on a bicycle, and I walked. I was a walking messenger from Geary Street 'way out near the ocean – and I delivered it myself. I came all the way back in and they said, "Where have you been all day?" And I said, "Well, I delivered the package." And they said, "Dopey! You were supposed to give it to somebody else who'd ship it out there."

Then I was assigned to the West Building which is an office building in downtown - the business section of San Francisco. I felt very important in my little uniform, and all we had to do was get into the elevators and go up to deliver them to the various offices; telegrams and every now and then we'd get packages which were called "R.E.A.", and we get a twenty-cent bonus out of it. So every time we'd see an R.E.A. come over we'd say, "Who's it for? Who's next?!?" If you'd get your R.E.A. - terrific!

****

It's possible he soon found out that bonuses and tips didn't always depend on the size of the package or the importance of the telegraph being delivered. Messenger boys were notoriously a favorite target of older homosexual men. Their tight uniforms on young, athletic bodies, their obvious need for money, all made them easy prey. Maybe this is where Harold got his introduction into the "gay" life of San Francisco (although this wasn't a word that would exclusively mean "homosexual" for many years yet).

According to one of his favorite stories, it was his delivery of a telegram to the San Francisco School of Ballet that set him on a more promising career path. He watched the students through the French doors as they took class. They did the splits, turned, flew through the air and he thought, "I can do that."

In retrospect, what did he have to lose? He had no other marketable skills besides his easy charm and wiry body. The theatrical life could give him a home and a career -- and respect. Being an American male involved in ballet during this time almost guaranteed you were considered homosexual anyway, so only known homosexual men were going to take on the stigma of being a "ballet dancer." If you were straight - or wanted to appear so - and drawn to a career in dance, you became a "hoofer" like Gene Kelly or Fred Astaire.

Ballet dancers in other countries might be given the same adoration and respect of trained athletes (which they really are), but in America they have always been considered "sissies." Harold quite possibly went through a period of conflict with his family and himself before enrolling in classes, but the desire to dance was too strong. Finally he was good at *something*.

If ballet was going to be his profession, he was in the right place. Very few dance schools of this period could compete with the excellent reputation of the San Francisco School of Ballet. Founded in 1933 by Adolph Bolm to supplement the San Francisco

Opera, both the school and the company very soon became the exclusive property of three dancing bothers from Portland, Oregon - Lew, William, and Harold Christensen. Their benevolent dictatorship would last over 30 years and turn out many of America's best native ballet dancers... who would then usually leave for New York City's greener dance pastures.

At first Harold kept his messenger job during the day and took classes at night at a small, sleazy ballet school run by Guy Aldon, a deaf-mute dance instructor whose classes catered to transvestites -- male prostitutes and female impersonators in the local drag shows. It wasn't long, however, before Harold was offered a scholarship at the San Francisco School of Ballet and found himself in the strict classes of the Christensen brothers.[1]

Harold's technique and stage presence improved rapidly under their disciplined tutelage, but his free and easy approach to ballet must have caused havoc in their classes. To the Christensen's, ballet was a religion; you prepared for performance and approached the stage like a priest preparing to celebrate Mass. Heck, Harold just wanted to have *fun*. Even later in life when he was more appreciative of the strictness needed to prepare a dancer for a career in ballet, he still couldn't help making it fun. That was just his nature. After all, if it wasn't fun, why do it? Even before giving up his day-job as a messenger boy, he was already feeling the thrill of performing:

One time I was delivering a telegram and was waiting for the elevator. I was alone on the landing, so I was practicing my turns. In the middle of a triple pirouette, the elevator doors opened to reveal a carload of people who just kind of looked at me as I finished in fourth position.

****

[1]Some listings have him studying with Theodore Kosloff first, but the above was Harold's story to me.

William, Lew and Harold Christensen at groundbreaking for new San Francisco ballet school facilities, 1982

Photo from San Francisco Opera Ballet 1939-40 souvenir program

And Now The Brides - 1940
(Harold is standing in right back group; 4th from l.)

(left) Harold standing outside San Francisco Opera House, 1939
(below) First full-length production of *Swan Lake* in America; choreographed by William Christensen and financed by San Francisco Tchaikovsky Foundation for the Tchaikovsky Centennial in 1939. (The Prince is danced by Lew Christensen. Harold - as Prince's Companion - is supporting dancer in arabesque to right of photo.)

1939 San Francisco World's Fair

(left) Dedication ceremonies - 1937   *(right)* view of the fair from San Francisco

(left) One of the most-visited spots on the Gayway, the **Temple of Nudity**

(below) Another popular attraction, an exhibition of incubator babies

The spectacular Courtyard of the Flowers

The United States was rapidly approaching its entrance into World War II, but as a last hurrah it was hosting not one, but two, World's Fairs. The best-known was located in New York, but the other was taking place at Treasure Island (now a US Naval base), in the San Francisco bay and had the more distinctive title of the "Golden Gate International Exposition." Harold was moonlighting as a barker/dancer in the amusement park at a small, ethnic restaurant (the Estonian Gardens), and ironically the whole amusement area was dubbed "The Gayway". (Although "gay" may not have had the meaning it has today, it's still a fair assumption that a teenaged male ballet-dancer could find more than a game of ring-toss there.) The World's Fair had given the Bay Area's economy a substantial shot in the arm, and many of Harold's friends also found excitement and employment there. A man-made island had been built to house the extravaganza, and the brand-new Bay Bridge was opened to handle the traffic. Harold would often refer to this colorful time in his life for his program bios. Looking at the old photos and newsreels, I can only guess it must have been quite an experience.

Exciting as it was, the job at Treasure Island lasted only a few months. By late1939 the San Francisco Opera Ballet went on an ambitious tour that began in Medford, Oregon and then traveled to Seattle, Washington and Victoria, Canada, Salt Lake City and Logan, Utah and finished in Phoenix, Arizona. Performing the waltzy *In Vienna and* in the festive, crowd-pleasing *Coppelia*, (America's first full-length production, where he alternated between being a "Village Boy" and the "Automatron-Drummer") Harold got his first taste of touring. In February of 1940 the WPA even sponsored a tour to Oklahoma City, where Harold again danced *Coppelia* and *In Vienna*. The successful tours were a major image boost for the young company and Harold's star was beginning to shine on the local dance horizon when suddenly the famous Ballet Russe de Monte Carlo swept into town.

It's difficult now to imagine the effect a company like Ballet Russe could have on a young dancer who had only recently been out of the San Francisco Bay Area. Without television in most homes, people had seen ballet only in movies or local dance school recitals. Even the word "ballet" sounded exotic, and Ballet Russe exploited every bit of mythology ever to come out of *The Red Shoes*. Originally formed from a group of dancers exiled in Europe by the Russian Revolution, the company worked hard to maintain an illusion of old-world glamour by constantly touring its travel-weary performers in a repertory of shopworn ballets; going from one side of America to the other; taking an eight-week break, and then starting all over again. As the original European dancers left the company from injuries and exhaustion, replacements would be picked up at any of the local dance schools; a quick name change and a plain Mary Smith might become a "Maria Smitovicha" or a Hank Brown, "Henri Banoff". The managers encouraged, sometimes even insisted, on new dancers creating a "European" stage name to cover the fact that the company was becoming more Americanized every year. Few European dancers could get through the war-time restrictions on travel, and nearly every American dancer was anxious to become a member of the world-famous Ballet Russe de Monte Carlo. Even James Starbuck, a premier danseur for the Christensen brothers, had left with "the Russians" after their last San Francisco tour. Harold had seen the company perform and was wild to join. Beginning a long habit of feigning illnesses to cover his real motives, he skipped out on a scheduled lecture-demonstration given by William Christensen to try his luck with the Russian company.

The story of his "audition" was one he would tell over and over throughout the years. Sneaking backstage with the help of a friendly doorman, he impulsively knocked on the dressing room door of the great choreographer-dancer, Leonide Massine. "Vhat do you vant?!" demanded the angry, disheveled Massine as he threw open the door. "I want to dance for you!" replied the cocky teen-ager. With a few muttered curses in Russian, Massine called to Roland Guerard, a soloist of the company, with orders to run the impetuous kid through a few paces. After taking Harold backstage and ordering him to do a series of pirouettes and jumps, Roland knocked on Massine's door and said simply, "Hire him."

Ballet Russe was already packing to leave for Los Angeles, where they would perform at the Hollywood Bowl and make two ballet "shorts" for Warner Brothers Studios. A few hours later Harold had packed his own bags, said good-bye to his family, and was on a train south to join them.

While the nation was preparing for war and other guys his age were thinking about joining the armed services; Harold was joining the Ballet Russe de Monte Carlo.

BALLET RUSSE de MONTE CARLO   HOLLYWOOD BOWL, CALIF

Ballet Russe at the Hollywood Bowl - July 1940

ON THE MOVIE LOT

Scenes in the Warner Brothers Studios during the filming of "Cafe Parisien" and "Capriccio Espagnol", the first ballet films made in Hollywood, featuring in lavish technicolor the Artists of the Ballet Russe de Monte Carlo.

Ballet Russe filming a version of *Gaite Parisienne* at the Warner Brother Studios immediately after Harold joined them. He would remember that he was thrown into the film at the last moment as a waiter, carrying a tray across the set. The cameraman focused for a moment on him, leading the older dancers to complain angrily , "Vhy new kid get close-up? He not even in ballet!"

CHAPTER 2: 1940-45
BALLET DAYS

By late 1941 Harold was officially a *corps de ballet* dancer for the Ballet Russe de Monte Carlo. For this exalted position he was earning about as much as a ditch digger of the same period; a starting salary of $22.50[1] (topping off at $45.00) a week for ten months per year of non-stop travel and dancing, plus paying for his own hotel rooms, tights and shoes. Besides a three-week holiday vacation (unpaid, of course), the annual two-month hiatus (also unpaid) would be the dancers' only real break from the drudgery of constant touring. Since it was nearly impossible for them to save any money during the touring year, they would usually take out loans on their next contract to see them through the off-season. In this way they always "belonged" to the company, which in turn fed off their youth and vitality. From the outside, it seemed like a glamorous life, especially to a young kid from Daly City. Once on the inside, however, it was literally "hell on wheels."

The Ballet Russe dancers may have looked like royalty when posed for their advertisement photos, but they lived like impoverished gypsies. Usually they traveled by train, performing eight shows a week. First-year dancers always took the upper berths, and the train left them off at their destinations so early there was no time to see where they were in the morning. They would be in and out of each town so quickly they'd get lost on their way to the theaters. Often they weren't even sure what city they were in until they checked the itinerary.[2] Meals were taken in desperation -- whenever and whatever possible. With no health odes for restaurants, they'd eat at any greasy-spoon café open after performances and trust their generally healthy constitutions to get them through.

---

[1] Lincoln Kirsten's letter to the editor; *The American Dancer,* May 1940 (see *Appendix A*)
[2] *Reminiscences II of Ballet Russes Dancers*

In a few large cities (Chicago, Detroit, etc.) there might be the luxury of spending a few days in the same hotel. Otherwise, it was on and off the train to one-night stands for weeks on end, with no limit in the number of times you would dance in an evening or what roles you would perform.

****

And here I step outside the narrative for a story of my own. As small-town high school students in 1963, my best friend, Donna Henry (Harter) and I, both avid members of the drama-dance class, were assigned to act as escorts to a visiting ballet troupe. Our job was to show them the stage, direct them to their dressing rooms, and be their "go-fers" for the evening. Since Red Bluff Union High School had the only real theatrical stage in town, it had become a regular stop on the Northern California Community Concert Series tours -- always a treat for us budding thespians. Every year we waited anxiously for the new season's list to be announced.

For those of you who grew up in urban areas, the Community Concert series was created to provide small towns like ours with a taste of the arts. Depending on how much money the area's committee was able to raise, they'd be able to book a series of performers ranging from single concert pianists (the least expensive) to larger dance companies (the most expensive.) For our dance selection that year we had a tiny company led by a former Premier Danseur of the Ballet Russe, by then a ballet instructor, his wife and two of their top students. Donna and I, stage-struck adolescents that we were (hadn't our drama instructor studied with Martha Graham?), went nearly speechless from shock to find that one of the performers was only *seventeen years old*. At fifteen-and-a-half, we considered ourselves mere nothings at the feet of this Professional Artist, and she made it quite clear there would be no teenage camaraderie between us.

The four dancers sniffed at the stage which we'd always thought so grand, and were less than thrilled to find their "dressing rooms" would be the second floor art room. We explained that the principal had considered the high, adjustable art desks to be more appropriate for their make-up needs than the conventional student desks in the classrooms directly across the hall from the stage. They accepted the situation with the world-weary attitude of combat veterans and began setting up their traveling kits. They would dress in the student restrooms down the hall, put on make-up sitting on high, metal stools at drafting tables, and then run up and down a flight of stairs for their entrances and costumes changes. *C'est la vie.*

The performance, as I remember, went only moderately well. There were several missteps and one delayed entrance that obviously had the Great Man seething. Right after the final curtain call, Donna and I rushed to the art room to help the company clean up, only to find our teen-aged ballerina in tears. Homesick, in pain from a blistered foot and crushed by the tongue-lashing she was getting from her director; she threw her toe shoes across the room and collapsed sobbing on her desk. We two theater neophytes stood enthralled. This was so much better than the performance we'd seen on stage!

At another desk, the director's wife calmly covered her face with cold cream looking thrilled the criticism wasn't being directed at *her*. The other male dancer was bustling about, folding costumes and trying to keep as far away from the line of fire as possible. I was guessing he'd seen this performance before.

Somehow we got them out the door and gave them directions to the only coffee shop in town open that late. They would drive to an even smaller town seventy miles north for another performance the next night. We didn't realize it at the time, but Donna[1] and I had just seen the lifestyle of the Ballet Russe .

[1] Let it be noted this is the same Donna Henry who won a 2nd Award that year in the annual Shakespeare Festival held, coincidentally, at CSU-Chico. (As usual, I came home empty handed.)

Dancers had no medical care or insurance; if you were sick or injured it was your own tough luck. Dancers would perform with injured bodies and raging fevers rather than risk being left behind in a strange city, alone and flat broke. The company was so notoriously stingy that once (in 1938), when the company was stuck onboard the train in a Mt. Shasta snowstorm, it tried to dock the dancers for the time they were snowbound. Only a threatened strike by the entire company restored the paychecks.

Somehow, only Alexandra Danilova managed to handle it all without complaints. At 7am the company's *prima ballerina* would be beautifully dressed and camera-ready as they pulled into the station, while her supporting dancers poured off the train looking like roadkill. Harold was her special pet from the first trip, and could sit with "Choura" (her pet name) for hours on the train as she taught him to speak Russian, the *lingua franca* of the group.

As for Massine, the great man held himself aloof from the dancers that adored and feared him. Sergei Denham may have owned Ballet Russe and Sal Hurok's name may have been forever connected with its booking, but Leonid Massine *was* Ballet Russe through this period-- the heart and soul of the company. He would work them at all hours in this pre-unionized time. If the theatre was closed, they would rehearse on hotel dance floors, in hallways, on trains, wherever there was space to move an arm or leg. If a dancer looked like they were on the verge of fainting, he would bring them back to life with a bite of food or a sip of gin, and they would go on dancing. And maybe, like throwing a dog a bone, he would tell them they did well.

And maybe, later, they would get to dance better roles.

Ballet Russe de Monte Carlo

with Lubov Roudenkov as The Small Fry in Massine's *The New Yorker*, 1940
(photo by Maurice Seymour)

Labyrinth (photo from 1942 Ballet Russe souvenir

HAROLD LANG, ANNA ISTOMINA, LEILA CRABTREE, MILADA MLADOVA
SONIA WOICIKOWSKA, ALEXANDER GOUDOVITCH

As the "Jockey", leading the Cakewalk in *Saratoga*, 1941

Tamara Toumanova in *Saratoga*

(photos from Mr. Lang's personal colletion)

Another of the dancers in the company was Tamara Toumanova, one of the famous "baby ballerinas." Like Danilova, she had been performing professionally since her early teens, and Harold insisted on giving me a photo of her when I went through his collection. He said she was impossible but adorable, something I thought of when I ran across the following from `H. Allen Smith's *Life In A Putty Knife Factory*:

Through the intercession of a friend I was able to arrange a luncheon date with a girl named Tamara Toumanova, ballerina with the Ballet Russe de Monte Carlo. Tamara is pronounce "tomorrow," as tomorrow is pronounced in my native Illinois, or tuhmorra. Tamara is a striking girl -- sort of a small Zorina. She talks at a fearful clip and is all full of animation, and she dilate her nostrils a lot, the way Valentino used to do in the silent movies to indicate he had ants in his pants.

I told Tamar I was a little on the idiot side, that this fluff-and-thistledown style of dancing always struck me as being silly; that these here-we-go-gathering-nuts-in-May dancers impressed me as less graceful than a heel-and-toe dancer, and would she be so kind as to instruct me in the art? Would she explain it to me so I'd be able to appreciate it?

Well, she made a noble effort. She took a specific piece of ballet business-- a thing called "The Labyrinth." It had been created especially for her by Salvador Dali. The way she explained it, Salvador Dali dreamed up the story, then got together with Leonide Choreographer, the eminent massine. Well, Leonide Choreographer found some music that would fit the story and then he got Tamara and they worked out the movements, and all the time Dali was designing costumes and sets and when it was finished, there it was. Of course, said Tamara, I really should have seen it to appreciate it. She mentioned it was full of pigeons, roosters, dragons and dolphins.

That was a little too heady for me-- too big a dose to be taken all at once-- so I got her away from ballet talk for awhile. She said that she dislikes her first name-- Tamara. The reason she dislikes it is that there are three or four other gals going around using the name Tamara. "I tried to cot off Tamara and be only one name Toumanova," she said, "but it would not work."

Tamara is a Russian name, so I asked her its equivalent in America-- the American name which corresponds to Tamara.

"Susie," she said. "Is Susie."

We drank some coffee and then she made a valiant try of explaining ballet some more. She talked about "grand jetes" and "tours en l'air" and "arabesques" and "acembles" (sic), providing the spelling of same. And she talked about "entre-chats."

An "entre-chats" is where the dancer jumps straight up in the air as high as he can go and, while in the air, begins wagging his legs so his feel cross and uncross, keeping it going until he hits the floor again. Here was something I could remember having seen. She spoke of "entre-chats" as though "entre-chats" were something out of this world. I tried to get myself into an appreciative frame of mind because I wanted so much to appreciate an "entre-chat," but I couldn't do it. Remembering the "entre-chats" I'd seen, I could only think, "What a hell of a thing for a grown man to be doing!"

Tamara went on to say that some men can "entre-chat" ten times, meaning that they can wag their legs that many times in a single jump. Women never get beyond six.

"Ten times," she said. "That is for the men. We do not try-- the girls. We do not try after six. The men try to go better than ten sometimes and they almost break the legs. They hit the floor and the feet are still going, and that is bad. A girl can come down on the toes and not break the legs, but not the men."

****

It didn't take long before Harold began getting restless; tired of the constant touring. There also seemed to be a lack of good roles for a short American boy, outside of being one of the original cowboys in Agnes de Mille's "Rodeo." Strangely enough, being part of that classic American ballet was something he never wanted to talk about.

A small, jazzy performance as one of the "Small Fry" in a Massine ballet called *The New Yorker* could have been the kind of part he was best suited for, but the Walter Terry review could hardly have been worse:

WALTER TERRY'S REVIEW OF "NEW YORKER"
BALLET RUSSE DE MONTE CARLO

<u>NY Herald Tribune</u> - Oct. 19, 1940

Massine's "New Yorker" Dance to Music of George Gershwin

Inventions of Caricaturists Supply Characters for Ballet Russe's Offering

The news this morning is grim, for it must be reported that the Ballet Russe de Monte Carlo took a nose-dive Friday evening into one of the worst ballets that it has been my misfortune to see in a long time. Leonide Massine's "The New Yorker" to a Gershwin score jumbled its way across the stage of the Fifty-First Street Theater in a production cursed with bad choreography, poor dancing and feeble humor. The idea, one imagines, was to bring to life the familiar characters in the New Yorker's drawings and to satirize gaily the foibles of smart New York. Yes, the Little King of Mr. Soglow was there, a Helen Hokinson woman heaved about and Steig's Small Fry tossed themselves around, but they were only poor imitations of the original.

****

But Massine was still determined to create an American ballet classic that would top *Rodeo*, and *Saratoga* would be another chance for both his choreography and Harold's career as a soloist. With a storyline about a day at the famous Florida racetrack, *Saratoga* gave Harold a chance to show off his dazzling technique as the "Jockey," where his short stature (so inconvenient for partnering) wasn't a problem. Leading the entire company in a photo of the "Cakewalk," Harold looked like a cat that swallowed the canary. If so, the reviews were enough to make him choke on it. Once again America's foremost dance critic Walter Terry was less than impressed with the production:

WALTER TERRY'S REVIEW OF "SARATOGA"

BALLET RUSSE DE MONTE CARLO

<u>NY Herald Tribune - Oct. 20, 1941</u>

A pretentious premiere flopped. An unpretentious debut rang the bell. These two events occurred last week when the Ballet Russe de Monte Carlo proved with "Saratoga" that a bad ballet is still bad no matter how lavish the production, and when Sybil Shearer bowed in as a solo artist at the Carnegie Chamber Music Hall and proved that really fine dancing, simply presented, can be theatrically exciting.

The "Saratoga" case is pretty tragic from many points of view. Firstly, Leonide Massine, its creator, has not had a hit ballet in several seasons. Russian ballet must have its successful novelties if it is to survive, for although the balletomanes will come back again and again for "Swan :Lake," the general public requires that its dance theater keep abreast of the times. Massine, as artistic director of the Monte Carlo company, does not have to prove his undeniable skill, but he does have to prove that skill is of the present as well as of the past. "Saratoga," as I suggested in my initial review, is by no means a hopeless work. The costumes are lovely, the set good, and much of the dancing is gay, but the Weinberger score is such trash that the choreographer must have been hard put to devise movement for its measures and the dancers equally exhausted with putting life into a work so musically uninspired. Alexandria Danilova and Fredric Franklin, two of ballet's great stars, deserve a ballet worthy of their talents, and although they sparkled frantically, even their theatrical genius could not save "Saratoga."

****

The failure of *Saratoga* was the last straw. Finally he understood there was never going to be enough roles outside the corps of Ballet Russe for him. Besides, Ballet Theatre was the future of dance in America, and Harold knew he had to be part of it.

Ballet Theatre was a unique company from the beginning. Unlike most ballet companies that are formed to showcase a choreographer's work or a national dance style, Ballet Theatre -- in true American fashion -- simply wanted the best of *everything* and wanted it <u>*immediately*</u>. To make matters as complicated as possible, the original plan had the company split into three separate groups, with an English, Russian, and American wing.[1] Each group would have its own choreographers who would call on a common ensemble of dancers for their works. Since the Russians at that time held first place in the world of ballet, it was decided to have four Russian choreographers, three for the English group and only one for the Americans.

[1] Originally there was a "Negro unit" which presented just one work; "Black Ritual" by Agnes de Mille.

Ballet Theatre was taking chances, concentrating on young performers and choreographers, and making the older, established companies seem outdated. At first the Ballet Russe downplayed the new competition; it wouldn't last beyond the first season (1940) they predicted. Like so many other "American" attempts at creating ballet, it could never live up to its own enthusiastic goals. However, when it not only lasted but began showing up in advertisements on Ballet Russe's own programs, the outcome looked less certain. Young, American-born dancers who had "Russianized" their names began thinking that it was possible to have a career as "Mary Smith" after all. Harold had never bothered to change his name anyway.[1] He was totally American and tailor-made for energetic, masculine roles in ballets like *The New Yorker* and *Rodeo*, and maybe he would have better luck finding roles in a truly American company. He had already taken classes in New York with many of the Ballet Theatre dancers and was friends with members of the company. Why not make the same kind of cold-call that had landed him in the Ballet Russe?

When I was with the Ballet Russe de Monte Carlo and we had a summer lay-off. Ballet Theatre had gone to glamorous Mexico City for their rehearsals and they did a season down there, too. I had friends in the company and I didn't want to stay in hot New York, so I jumped on a Greyhound and it took me five days and five nights to get to Mexico, then on a Mexican bus to Mexico City. I checked into the little rooming house where some of the Ballet Theatre kids were staying and found out where Gerry Sevastianov -- who was married to Irina Baronova, their ballerina -- where they were staying. I went up to this house they had rented, pushed my way through the garden and went up the stairs to the front door, opened up the door -- didn't even knock – and there they were in an embrace on the sofa -- dressed, but in an embrace. Gerry said, "What are you doing here? Get out! Who are you?" I said, "I just came from New York City. I'm with the Ballet Russe and I'd like to join Ballet Theatre," and Irina said, "Oh no, daahling, let him stay. Let him talk. I saw him dance with the Ballet Russe. He's very

[1]He'd joke about the Nutcracker's Russian Trepak -danced by "Katcharoff, Goudovitch... and <u>Lang</u>."

good." So I said, "I have a good technique. I love your company and I would like to be in it." Gerry said, "Don't be silly. Right here in Mexico City we have four boys who are paying their own way to be with us. We do not give them salary, we have too many people." I was doing some small parts with Ballet Russe, so with a sad heart I left and went back on tour.

****

As the 1943-44 season opened he found himself on the train with Ballet Russe when a telegram arrived:

We were on tour and I got a telegram signed "Gerry Sevastianov, " just saying, "When are you coming to join us?" Just that. So I went to Ivan Ivanovitch who was our ballet master and said, "I'm sick. I must get off the train." It was just at the point where we were starting to sign contracts again for another year, and he said, "Oh no, you can't leave. Impossible!" And I said, "But I've got smallpox!" I'd taken aspirin, which makes me break out. "Ivan Ivanovitch, do you want the whole company to be sick, not to be able to open anyplace?" This was on the train after Pittsburgh, we were going to another date. He said, "No, no -- you sick boy. You go back to New York, we send for you later. Good-bye."

So the train stopped and I found my way back to New York. Ballet Theatre was in session there and I went backstage during their evening performance because the stage doorman knew me from Ballet Russe, and there were Anthony Tudor and Nora Kaye. I walked up to them and said "Hello." They said, 'Oh, how wonderful. Thank God," and they both hugged me. "You are with us now.

The 1943-44 Ballet Theatre souvenir program had a small photo of Harold with this brief biographical note:

Born in Daly City, California. Studied dancing in San Francisco
Opera School of the Ballet and later joined the San Francisco
Opera Ballet. For two years he appeared with Ballet Russe de
Monte Carlo, and this is his first season with Ballet Theatre.

At heart, Harold remained a Ballet Theatre performer for the rest of his life.

Ballet Theatre: 1943-44

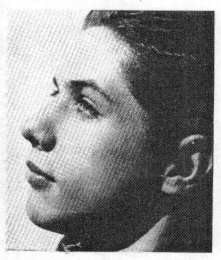

HAROLD LANG

Balanchine's "Waltz Academy" - 1944
(L to R: Fernando Alonso, Albia Kavan, Harold Lang)

DANCE magazine cover, April 1945

Graduation Ball

HAROLD LANG

Program photo 1944-45 season

He had picked a good time to leave Ballet Russe. Although the company would soldier on for another twenty years, the glory days were over. From now on its dancers would be mostly American; just a few of the original European performers, with no real home to return to after the war, would return year after year. The company was their only home and family, but through them the memories and traditions of the Imperial Ballet would be passed down to other generations of dancers. Massine himself would choreograph for *both* companies (not finishing his Ballet Russe career until 1954.) But Harold, restless at heart though he was, had finally found a ballet company and a hometown that suited him.

Harold was by nature a New Yorker. He was born and would die on the West Coast, but only in New York City could he really feel like *Harold Lang*. Now, sharing an apartment with two other male dancers that became notorious for its parties and gay coterie, Harold settled into discovering the glamour and the sleaze of the Big Apple. Broadway was calling, and already he was thinking that maybe Ballet Theatre was just a stepping-stone to "real" theatre... maybe even movies.

By this time he'd accepted the fact that he wasn't cut out to be a premier danseur. Those roles were for tall, conventionally handsome men and Harold would never top five feet, five inches. Being so short meant he could partner only the most petite ballerinas, and the "brash youngster" look that later worked so well for him in musical comedy didn't suit the classical male roles in ballet he wanted.

Also, Harold hated being controlled, and ballet companies are disciplined. He was young and arrogant-- not to mention extremely sensitive about his appearance, especially onstage. Even in Ballet Theatre there was no opportunity to choose a role... or costume, as he told me in an interview:

There was one ballet called "Mademoiselle Angot ." Massine had this costume designer that just went out of his skull designing this. I couldn't even follow the story line and I was in it! Massine danced in it, Egravsky, Janet Reed, but I don't know what I was.

They put me in this weird costume and all I did was march out and do a few little semi-ethnic Russian steps. It was all just pageantry. Finally the costumer came up to me and strapped cymbals on the insides of my knees. And that was the height of... I-don't-know-what! I said, "I'm not wearing those" and off I threw them. And a weird hat! It really wasn't dancing. I just __hated__ that ballet.[1]

****

Ballet Theatre may have had a permanent home in New York, but that didn't mean they were completely tour-free. Their annual dates in the Midwest helped pay the bills, and Harold hadn't been with them long before he found himself on the road again.

The country may have been at war by the time Harold joined Ballet Theatre, but it was still a productive time in the life of the company. During the 1943-44 season they were premiering works like *Capriccio Espanol* and *Dim Luster*, and, in spite of severe wartime rationing, managed not only to perform regularly in New York, but also to tour. Considering the shortages in fuel that had even armed service personnel hitching rides home for their leaves, the notion of hauling an entire ballet company cross-country -- people, scenery, costumes and all -- is astounding.

And the dancers. Besides Harold, Michael Kidd and Andre Eglevsky joined the company in 1943. Already there were Anton Dolin, Jerome Robbins, Hugh Laing; ballerinas Alicia Markova (born Alice Marks), Nora Kaye, and Alicia Alonso. Lucia Chase (whose personal fortune helped found the company) was performing, and would

---

[1] *The ballet - a well-deserved flop - had a story about a girl, engaged to a barber, who falls in love with an artist, who loves an aristocrat. The Harold Lang Archives (which sprang from the research for this book) contains a December 14, 1943 Ballet Theatre program from Des Moines, Iowa listing Harold in this as a "Hussar."*

continue to dance even small, character roles while directing the company for many years. It was a young, proud, multi-cultural *American* company.[1]

It was January, 1944 and Ballet Theatre was on tour in Chicago when rehearsals began for "Fancy Free." Thanks to Sol Hurok's insistence that the company needed new works with more popular *American* appeal (ala *Billy the Kid* and *Rodeo*), a young *corps de ballet* member, Jerome Robbins, had been given the chance to stage a one-act ballet with the warning that it had better not strain the company's budget. A small cast, minimal setting and costumes... it didn't matter. Jerry Robbins was so hungry to have his work staged he would have choreographed it naked on a bare floor.

For an original (and relatively inexpensive) score he turned to a young pianist-composer who had accompanied the company ballet classes until he got dismissed for playing Shostakovich during plies -- Leonard Bernstein. Company designer Oliver Smith would do the sets and costumes, and the cast would come from the young dancers in the corps de ballet. Since the company was scheduled for a nationwide tour, nearly all the choreography and rehearsal (outside of a brief time before opening night in New York City) would have to be done on the road. Meanwhile, Leonard Bernstein would be composing the score, recording it on phonograph disks with the help of his friend Aaron Copeland, and mailing the records to Robbins at whatever the next stop on the tour happened to be.

It wasn't an easy job. The dancers would listen to the records and rehearse early in the morning on nightclub stages or anywhere else they could find in a strange city. Then they would take company class, attend any extra rehearsal called for by the

---

[1] *It also had many young American men - obviously in the best of physical health - dancing in tights and mascara instead of serving their country overseas. Explaining his non-participation in such a patriotic time must have been a challenge. When performing in "Fancy Free" at a military base, Harold was pleased to be mistaken for a regular sailor when in costume off-stage, but I can't help wondering what Harold's father (who died in 1949) felt about his son dancing instead of fighting.*

sloppiness in performances or emergency cast changes in the regular touring productions, and perform in the evening before moving on to the next town. Rex Cooper, one of the original dancers, was replaced and given a job as the bartender. Nobody knew if it would be ready in time.

The finishing touches were put on the ballet in Hollywood, the last stop on the tour. Robbins was working on Harold's solo when he noticed Harold easily stretching in a full split. Could he land there from a double air-tour? Harold shrugged and tried, nailing the move on the first attempt. Jerry laughed and told him he now had the opening movement of the solo, a movement that would never fail to bring down the house.

Opening night -- April 18, 1944. No one except company director Lucia Chase had seen the ballet, which had been composed, choreographed designed and danced by a team of artists all under twenty-five years old. Only Bernstein's name was familiar. A month earlier he had taken over the podium of the New York Philharmonic from Bruno Walter on half-an-hour's notice and his conducting had been praised in every major newspaper the next morning. Just a week earlier his "Jeremiah" symphony had received the Critic's Award for the best new American piece of the year, and many in the audience that night were there mainly to hear the new Bernstein score. No one knew what the evening would mean in the history of American ballet.

The curtain opened on a seedy bar and street. Three sailors and two city girls are out having a night on the town. Time after time the audience roared with laughter. This dancing wasn't just fabulous, it was *funny*. When it was over, the exhausted, amazed cast came out on stage to take their bows and couldn't get off again; they took curtain call after curtain call. An orchestra recording of the opening night performance had a band of recorded applause that lasted nearly as long as the score itself. Harold would later say it seemed to go on *forever*-- and suddenly, they were all stars.

Original cast:
(l. to r.)
Jerome Robbins,
John Kriza,
Harold Lang,
Janet Reed,
Muriel Bentley

Harold, in the opening move of his solo.

"Action photo", taken during 1945 performance

Signed still photo

Performing *Fancy Free* at a USO show for an audience of real sailors, where Harold was nearly denied entrance because he "didn't have his military papers"

Action Photos
(above) betting for drinks
(below) fight scene

CHAPTER 3: 1945-50

BROADWAY, AT LAST!

Suddenly, Harold found himself extremely desirable. In Daly City he'd been an ugly duckling but he'd been transforming himself into swan material, muscle by muscle and feature by feature, since his days in San Francisco Ballet. True, he couldn't do much about his size, but anything that could be improved on, was. The nose became smaller, the skin was kept as clear as possible -- considering the nightly use of theatrical greasepaint. New York City decided he was a hot commodity. People wanted to love him, and he was ready to let them.

If you're going to be a top-notch seducer of men and/or women, probably your number one asset is not to give a damn. Harold had that one nailed. As Helen Gallagher put it, he was totally incapable of real love.

The second-most valuable asset for a great seducer is the ability to *seem* like you're able to love; in other words, to put on a good performance. With both these skills in place, a body that looked terrific in a sailor suit, and a boyish smile what just melted your heart, Harold was ready to take on New York's best.

He'd grown up in a poor home, but suddenly rich lovers were fighting over the chance to spend money on him. His family background was middle-class, but any night he could be sharing a bed with someone whose family connections went all the way into the White House. His education may have been mediocre, but he was learning a lot from the Ivy League men he was hanging out with these days.

One man with all these attributes, Gore Vidal, may have been the most famous of his lovers, but it's hard to keep score. By his own admission he slept with just about anybody who was *anybody* in those days, and had ongoing relationships with so many that he couldn't keep them from running into each other at the doorway. When things got too hot he'd high-tail it back to home to "visit his mother" for a few weeks. In those days it was harder to follow a fleeing lover to California, and most New Yorkers would be hard-pressed to find Daly City on a map. When he felt tempers had cooled off and the coast was clear, he'd slide back into Manhattan and start all over again.

Broadway 1945

There were thirty-four legitimate theater houses in New York City, and thirteen were playing musicals. Tickets to all the shows were selling well on Broadway, and there were thirty-seven shows out on the road. It was a good time for theater. Television was still just an electronic toy with a fuzzy black-and-white screen that could never be a threat to flesh and blood performers.

One of the biggest hits of 1945 was a show that could have been Harold's big break. For the first time, a successful Broadway musical comedy was based on the plot of a one-act ballet. *On The Town,* inspired by the success of *Fancy Free,* opened three days after Christmas 1944 and soon became the jazzy favorite of a wartime public. Harold would have sold his soul to have played his *Fancy Free* character on the musical stage, but with very little acting experience and limited singing ability he wasn't even in the running. After five years of constant rehearsing, touring and performing he was tired and began to think about leaving Ballet Theatre (although he would continue to appear occasionally as a "guest artist" on tours until the late 1950s):

It was at the Met. I'd been on tour, performing and rehearing, and the union wasn't as strong then as it is now. It's like doing summer stock, where you rehearse one production during the day and give your all at night in a completely different production. You may have a Dutch accent during the day and a British one at night, and you get so screwed up! They were working me night and day. I was really exhausted; I really had to *push myself. Other people would be doing maybe three ballets a week and I was doing three a <u>night</u>! So John Alden Talbot - he was partners with Lucia in running the company - was standing in the wings one night and I thought, "Aha – I'll get him!"*

After our third ballet I just stumbled off and collapsed at his feet. They tried to revive me and I refused to open my eyes. Finally, "What happened? What happened?" They helped me up, and Alden was saying, "Oh my goodness!" I said, [voice drops plaintively] "It's just that I'm working so hard. I had to rehearse all day, do the three ballets tonight and we just got off tour and --- oohhhh." They had me in every single ballet! Lucine had just choreographed a ballet, I was in that, and right down the line every night.

That was the only time in my whole life I ever fainted and that was fake.

****

1945 Summer Stock season; Stamford, CT.

If he was going into musical theater, he needed legitimate acting experience. A summer stock season across the Hudson in Stamford, Connecticut playing in *The Spider*, *Over 21* and *Boy Meets Girl* padded his resume a little. He was also taking singing lessons from Keith Davis, vocal coach to the stars.[1] The Davis vocal technique was a way to bridge together all registers of the voice. He worked with each student to build a bridge between the low voice (chest) and the high voice (head) combining in the center to create a "mix." Harold practiced for hours in alleyways and vacant lots until he finally discovered his baritone, quit the company and was auditioning for Broadway musicals:

We'd been touring so strenuously that I decided to just not go out another year. I gave up the company and I was living there in New York at a playwright friend's apartment. I realized my

---

[1] According to Tom McKinney, a Houston-based instructor who carries on the technique, Mr. Davis had more Broadway Stars and "Tony" award winning singers in his studio than any other teacher in New York.

money was dwindling, because we didn't make that much. Well, we made good but I didn't save. I said, "Oh, I've got to get a job," and then this theatrical lawyer, Arnold Weisburger called me, took me out to lunch and said, "Would you be interested in doing a musical?" So I said "I guess so," so they put me in "Strauss" "[Mr. Strauss Goes To Boston"] and Balanchine choreographed. The dancing and my personal reviews were very favorable. The musical only lasted ten days, but I got good coverage in Time Magazine, Life magazine, so I was offered a musical right after that -- that was a hit!

****

Mr. Strauss Goes To Boston - Sept. 6, 1945

He invited his family in California to come out and see the show once it was up and running instead of opening night --- a major mistake because although the show did get up to Broadway after a try-out in Boston, it closed after only 10 days. (Helen Gallagher remarked, "It didn't deserve to last that long.") As Theatre Arts said [1], "...no amount of waltzing could redeem (it) from monumental boredom." On the plus side, TIME had mentioned Harold's name as one of the show's few saving graces.[2] A later program bio would have him describing the experience as a "mistake of youth." Two important relationships came into his life from the experience, however; his long friendships with choreographer George Balanchine and dance partner Helen Gallagher. Unhappy with his assigned partner, Harold had picked Helen out of the chorus line, not knowing it had been her dream to dance with him ever since she'd seen him in "Graduation Ball." It was one of the best choices he ever made; Helen was the perfect partner for him. Too bad Harold couldn't seem to keep anything perfect in his life. [3]

---

[1] 1945-46 issue
[2] Sep. 17, 1945
[3] Helen Gallagher would say later that she "fell in love with him at least seven or eight times" over the years, and even their friends who knew of his preferred sexual orientation had no doubt he loved her... in his fashion.

HAROLD LANG

Harold Lang, the premier dancer, studied dancing at the San Francisco Opera School of Ballet. He joined a touring ballet troupe five years ago, and has been trouping constantly since—two years with the Ballet Russe de Monte Carlo and two with the Ballet Theatre dancing important solos in "Fancy Free," "Bluebird," "Graduation Ball," "The Blue Danube" and "Carnival." As an actor he played in "Boy Meets Girl" and "Over 21" at the Stamford, Conn., Summer Theatre this summer.

BEGINNING AUGUST 13th FOR 5 WEEKS

FELIX BRENTANO

presents

"Mr. Strauss Goes To Boston"

A Romantic Comedy With Music

with

GEORGE RIGAUD · VIRGINIA MacWATTERS · RALPH DUMKE

RUTH MATTESON · EDWARD J. LAMBERT · JAY MARTIN · HAROLD LANG

Music by ROBERT STOLZ
Lyrics by ROBERT SOUR
Book by LEONARD L. LEVINSON
Based on an original story by
ALFRED GRUENWALD and GEZA HERCZEG
Choreography by GEORGE BALANCHINE
Production designed by STEWART CHANEY
Costumes by Walter Florell
Conductor ROBERT STOLZ
Production Staged and Directed by MR. BRENTANO

CHARACTERS IN ORDER OF APPEARANCE

POLICEMAN McGILLICUDY	BRIAN O'MARA
INSPECTOR GOGARTY	DON FISER
1st REPORTER	DENNIS DENGATE
2nd REPORTER	LARRY GILBERT
3rd REPORTER	JOSEPH MONTE
PEPI	FLORENCE SUNDSTROM
DAPPER DAN PEPPER	RALPH DUMKE
ELMO TILT	EDWARD LAMBERT
MESSENGER	FRANK FINN
JOHANN STRAUSS	GEORGE RIGAUD

GEORGE BALANCHINE

The word "choreographer" is at long last considered good usage by the grammarians who paint the houseboards for the musical comedy and revue productions.

A Russian ballet-master has legitimized the word by adding a new credit line, reading "choreography by George Balanchine" to the theatre program form.

Now no musical impresario can lightly undercut the standards set by Balanchine's choreography, and even the jealous guardians of the precision school of hoofing must look for richer comic invention and variety if they wish their tradition of six up and six down rhythms to survive. For George Balanchine, coming from the "highbrow" ballet world has set his mark on the commercial Broadway theatre.

For a young man in his middle 30's, his record of achievement is impressive. He is responsible for numerous smash hits including an edition of the "Follies," at least three Rodgers and Hart productions, "On Your Toes," "Babes in Arms," "I Married An Angel," "The Merry Widow" and "A Song of Norway." He has founded and developed an American Ballet company that can unblushingly lay claim to the finest ensemble dancers in the world outside of Russia, where a tradition of 200 years of ballet has produced the best ballet of all time.

inscription reads:

"To Mother dear and Al and Daddy – I love you and am always thinking of you.

Harold"

Harold was without a job and feeling the sting of having made his musical theatre debut in a total flop. Luckily, Ballet Theatre was willing to take him back. By November they were even allowing him to dance some of Hugh Laing's roles in an effort to keep him interested in staying "home", but the reviews he received when trying to replace the tall, elegant Laing were poor. Attempting Massine's original role in *Aleko* he was reportedly missing "the sinuous independence the part requires,"[1] although his shortcomings in the Laing roles were also blamed on insufficient rehearsal and poor planning by the company. Only in Jerome Robbins's *Interplay* was his dancing judged "exceptionally brilliant." Disappointment with his lack of success in the ballet roles he'd always wanted only strengthened his determination to give musicals another try.

Three To Make Ready - March 7, 1946

Not quite a musical but hopefully a more successful foot-in-the-door than *Mr. Strauss*, Harold landed a part in the revue *Three To Make Ready* in early 1946. He was cast on his dancing ability, but the vignettes also offered a chance to show off a little of his acting and singing talents. The show also introduced him to his first "dance-act" partner, Jane Deering. Together they had a stop-the-show number in "Barnaby Beach," which gave them the opportunity them to try pick up some extra cash by moonlighting in nightclubs after the show.

As "Deering and Lang" they headlined the famed Waldorf-Astoria Wedgewood Room in late 1946 and early 1947, as well as on television. No one seems to know what happened between them, but their partnership broke up as quickly as it began. Years later Harold would look at a picture of them together and say flatly, "That's a girl I used to dance with in a nightclub act. I forget her name." It wasn't in his nature to remember anything negative. It was easier to wipe the entire person from his memory.

The show itself had better luck. The star, Ray Bolger was the beloved Scarecrow from The Wizard of Oz, and other performers included Gordon MacRae, Bibi Osterwald, a brand-new Kaye Ballard and "guest artist" Arthur Godfrey. Bolger would do a number called "The Old Soft Shoe" that made the title of "hoofer" rank right up there with royalty. After a respectable 323 performances and a touring date in Chicago, Harold was back in New York making the audition rounds. But he was young and a hot property. He wouldn't stay unemployed for very long:

The composer and playwrights had seen me in "Three To Make Ready" and they wanted me in the show because it was about a touring ballet company. They had me written down as – "Shaunny O'Shea," I believe was the character I was supposed to play, and the composer wrote two songs for me. The lead – they didn't know who was going to play the lead -- was a surly, pushy fellow in the ballet company that wanted to become the top choreographer, so he's pulling all kinds of gimmicks to get there. The writers wanted me to try for the lead. I didn't know how to read the script so I'd say, "Oh-I-didn't-know-Sarah-that-you-were-in-this-room-practicing," you know, just like a parrot. And so the playwrights -- I had to audition for Jerry Robbins, who was the choreographer and George Abbot, who was the director -- they kept me up all night saying, "Well, how would you feel if your favorite dog had been run over?" Practically, Method! So I thought, "Oh, OH – that's how to act!!"

I had the audition about two days later in a dance studio, reading the script. I had them all crying with my love scene, rejecting the girl and stuff. So they said, "You're the lead.

Photo from May 5, 1946 television version of the ballet *Spectre De la Rose*, danced by Harold and Jane Deering to Gershwin's "Concerto in F."
The TV title was "Spectre de la Roseland."
(*Dance Screen & Stage*, June 1947)

Harold dancing Cossack solo from the same performance.
(*photo from his personal collection*)

Harold Lang and Jane Deering dance "There's Something On My Program"

(l.) photo from *Theatre World* 1945-46
(r) photo from *Dance Magazine* October 1946

Harold Lang and Jane Deering are the featured dancers of "Three To Make Ready" which stars Ray Bolger. Robert Sidney is credited with the choreography for this revue.

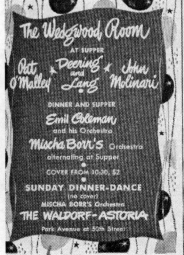

Ad from December 1946 *Playbill*

- 45 -

THREE TO MAKE READY is an evening made gay with dance. Besides Ray Bolger's inimitable exhibitions of footwork, there are Harold Lang and Jane Deering, seen above in a number called 'Barnaby Beach,' to contribute some light and fantastic toe work. Lang is from the Ballet Theatre, Miss Deering from *Are You With It?* and, before that, *Early to Bed*. The engaging settings against which they perform are the work of Donald Oenslager; the costumes are by Andre. The entire production, whose words are Nancy Hamilton's and music Morgan Lewis', was staged by John Murray Anderson.

Souvenir Program

HAROLD LANG

Harold Lang is making his Broadway theatrical debut in "Three To Make Ready" although he is a popular and familiar figure to balletomanes.

Harold, who skyrocketed to fame for his ebullient dancing and pantomiming as one of the sailors in the Ballet Theatre's production of "Fancy Free," began his career as a terpsichorean at the San Francisco World's Fair. A native of San Francisco, he was employed as a barker at Treasure Island. In his off hours he enrolled in a modern dance group class and rehearsed with the group to perform a Balinese Monkey dance at the Artists' Pavilion on the midway.

Before long he was a member of the Ballet Russe de Monte Carlo. Five seasons ago he made his New York bow with that company at the Metropolitan. He transferred allegiance to the Ballet Theatre, where he danced in Bluebird, Graduation Ball, Aleko and Carnaval.

Summer stock productions of Lynn Riggs' "Borned In Texas," "Once 21," "The Spider" and "Boy Meets Girl" gave him acting experience. As a choirboy at Grace Cathedral in San Francisco he received voice training at an early age.

Once when performing "Fancy Free," which later was expanded into "On The Town," for Navy hospitals, he was stopped from going backstage by officers who mistook him in his goblin garb for a bona fide tar.

Ray Bolger in "Three to Make Ready"

Look Ma, I'm Dancin' - Jan. 29, 1948

Most performers hope for just one good show in a year; but in 1948 Harold had two. *Look Ma, I'm Dancin'* was actually more successful as a vehicle for those involved and only semi-successful as a musical. Based on an idea by Jerome Robbins (who shared direction and choreography credits with George Abbott), the show starred the talented Nancy Walker (a huge hit as "Hildy" in the original cast of *On The Town*) and told the story of a wealthy beer-brewer's daughter so infatuated with the world of ballet that she buys herself a company of dancers so she can play "prima ballerina."

In addition to Nancy Walker, the show starred Harold (in the first of his brash "bad-boy" roles as "Eddie Winkler", choreographer-cad), Janet Reed (ballerina of the San Francisco Ballet and an old friend of Harold's), Alice Pearce (the only member of the original *On The Town* cast who would reprise their role in the film version) and Tommy Rall (another ex-Ballet Theatre dancer who would later play Harold's *Kiss Me, Kate* part in the film version.) The score of *Look Ma, I'm Dancin'* still has a cult following today, and "I'm The First Girl In The Second Row" is a favorite of chorus girls everywhere.

Running 188 performances on Broadway and a moderate tour, the musical was too good to be a failure but not good enough to be a real success. In the meantime, making the "original cast recording" (a set of 78rpms) was a thrill -- the first time he'd been recorded as a singer. Copies of the record set were soon sent to Daly City so everyone back home would know that Harold had become a *Somebody*.

Harold as "Eddy Winkler," choreographer for the "Russo-American Ballet Company" in *Look Ma, I'm Dancin'!*

Harold leads the company members in "Gotta Dance"

Romantic Triangle: *(left & center)* Harold with old San Francisco Ballet chum Janet Reed
(right) Harold with show's star and off-star romantic interest Nancy Walker

(left) Nancy shows off her technique *(center)* Nancy and Alice Pearce commiserate
(right) Alice Pearce and Harold share a drink *(photo courtesy of Fredrick Tucker)*

Kiss Me, Kate - December 30, 1948

Later in the year he was cast as the second male lead in the Broadway blockbuster hit, *Kiss Me, Kate*, which opened at the end of 1948 and would last on Broadway a phenomenal 1077 performances. The score contained some of Cole Porter's best songs at a time when many New Yorkers were calling Porter a has-been. So much has been written about this classic of the musical theater that I can only refer readers to the descriptions in the books I've listed in the bibliography. How Harold got the part might be another story entirely. Backstage gossip of inside connections and a "casting couch" being involved still lingers today, but by this time Harold's talent (although his singing was still a little raw) should have been enough to earn him the role.

However he got it, Harold's part ("Bill Calhoun") was tailor-made to his talents, complete with a show-stopping dance turn in "Too Darn Hot." He even had a solo written for him (after much prodding) by the great Cole Porter -- an inane little ditty that rhymed "Bianca" with "Sanka." The story of how it came to be written at all is one of those too-good-to-be-true Broadway tales:

Early in the rehearsals, Harold Lang, who had been hired to play Calhoun-Lucentio, became visibly perturbed over the fact that he had no solo. He was a well-established member of the American Ballet Theatre and as rehearsals progressed he became more and more unhappy. Cole sympathized with him, but for the moment was without a workable idea. Then, one evening after rehearsal he invited Lisa Kirk to go back to the Waldorf-Towers for a drink. As they stepped into the elevator, Cole tentatively began to whistle a tune. He stopped, started again and pushed on to the finish just as the elevator door opened for the forty-first floor. As Miss Kirk stepped out, she remarked she had never heard that tune before and asked what it was.

"It's Harold's number," Cole replied. He eventually called it "Bianca." He had written it between the first and forty-first floors. [1]

[1] p. 277 – Stuart W. Little, *Off-Broadway: The Prophetic Theater*

(l to r) Patricia Morison, Alfred Drake, Lisa Kirk, Harold Lang in "We Open In Venice"

Kiss Me, Kate was the first show to win a Tony Award as Best Musical. (Before that year, the category didn't exist.)

Harold LANG

Harold Lang, nimble-footed, graceful, lithe, literally danced his way across the country from his native California to Manhattan. Ever since he was a boy in Daly City, California, he had only one ambition—to dance—and he has never let any obstacle stand in his way.

After a period of training at the Opera Ballet School in San Francisco, Harold made his debut in, of all places, Logan, Utah, as the King of Dandies in Leonide Massine's ballet, "Beau Danube." Talent scouts spotted Harold and he was immediately engaged by the San Francisco Opera Ballet Company, which sent him on tour as soloist. Next came tours with the Monte Carlo Ballet Russe and the Ballet Theatre.

Harold's first dancing role in a Broadway show was scheduled to be in "Mr. Strauss Comes to Boston"; Harold was its lead dancer but since the play was short-lived, it was a rather disappointing beginning. Came an interim of stock in which Harold side-stepped dancing for a few months to play the juvenile leads in "Over 21," "Boy Meets Girl," and "The Spider," in Stamford, Connecticut.

But that time out served only to convince Harold that he wanted to be in song and dance shows. Two years ago, Harold Lang was the leading dancer in "Three To Make Ready," which starred Ray Bolger, and last season he was the romantic lead in "Look, Ma, I'm Dancin'." Recently, Harold danced at the Waldorf in the Wedgwood Room and appeared as guest artist with the Ballet Theatre.

Next to dancing, Harold Lang has a pet avocation, and that's raising French poodles. When he was dancing in "Three To Make Ready," his partner, Jane Deering, presented him with a toy poodle. Now Harold has three poodles and a chihuahua, and he's mighty proud of the ribbons they've won.

Harold's bio page from the souvenir program

This was *It*... the "Big Break", the show that would put him right up there in the Broadway star category.[1] Brooks Atkinson of The New York Times called him "versatile and attractive." His photo was in Life magazine and he was featured on Ed Sullivan's "Toast of the Town" television show four times between 1949 and 1951.[2]

Harold stayed with "Kiss Me, Kate" until May of 1950, nearly a year and a half. Considering this was a major Broadway hit (indeed, one of the hits of the century), most young performers would have hung onto such a plum role until closing night -- and then they would have gone out on the nation tour. According to a young man who ran into him after a performance, Harold "was very pleased to be in the show" and "exuded happiness and contentment." But Harold had a restless soul, and he thought there would

Set of "action stills" for a 1949 *Toast of the Town*.

These photos would be taken during rehearsal to help the lighting and cameramen prepare for the live television performance.

(also from Harold's personal collection)

from *Theatre Arts*, April 1949:

"Harold Lang defies gravity in *Kiss Me, Kate*"

---

[1] In the 2002 hit revival, Michael Berresse would publicly honor the memory of Harold Lang as he recreated the role of Bill Calhoun.

[2] Harold would later recall that the studio lights for early television made the set so hot that he nearly passed out from heatstroke during these rehearsals.

be lots of Broadway opportunities now that he was a star.

In the meantime, there was an opportunity to join the New York City Ballet for its summer performances in London. In spite of his success in "Fancy Free" Harold felt that he'd never really conquered the world of ballet. This would be a position of prestige, and besides - how could a dancer turn down a trip to perform in London for *George Balanchine*?

The New York City Ballet in London – 1950: "Price of Program -- Sixpence"

England was still recovering from the hardships of World War II when the New York City Ballet was invited to perform at Covent Garden in the summer of 1950. The tiny, plain programs were a result of a long paper shortage, and conditions were known going in to be Spartan. The Sadler's Wells (Royal) Ballet had been a hit the year before in America, though, and this was America's response.

Harold was signed on as a guest artist, a temporary member of the NYCB, in 1950. He had always enjoyed dancing with Balanchine, calling "Symphony in C" "a joy", and said:

I loved rehearsing with New York City Ballet because I'd taken so many classes in the studios it felt like home to me. I heard they wanted a new ballet for New York City season and they didn't have much money. So Balanchine said, "We need money for costumes." Somehow he got together with Jantzen bathing suit company and they donated bathing suits for all the boys and the girls. "Oh, bathing suits! I'll do ballet by beach. Swimming!" So he did and it worked out beautifully. I was a mosquito. Four boys were mosquitoes. Oh, it was marvelous. We were just wearing bathing trunks and four of us just did a zap-out, technical type of dance -- real fast and jazzy. Tanny [Tanaqil Le Clerq] was the one who was drowning, that was the adagio. It was done in classical form except it took place in bathing suits on a beach.

He may have been a mosquito, but he wasn't an opening night mosquito.[1] The premiere list of dancers lists Jerome Robbins, but not Harold. The ballet - jointly choreographed by Balanchine and Robbins - had been premiered in March of 1950, while Harold was still performing in *Kiss Me, Kate*. (Although he was probably taking company classes with Balanchine in the mornings and was present at the initial rehearsals.).

His old comrade from Ballet Theatre, Jerome Robbins, now a shining hope of NYCB and Balanchine's designated successor, seems to have turned a cold shoulder to the new Broadway star in the company. Although Harold had been one the stars in Jerry's first hit, *Fancy Free*, it was probably a given that their combined egos clashed in the workplace. Jerry was a perfectionist and a bully; Harold was hard-working but easy-going. Even as an instructor he wasn't a disciplinarian. ("Other teachers insist on black leotards for class," he'd joke. "Look at my classes - every color of the rainbow!") Harold and Jerry had spent time together in Ballet Theatre, *in Look Ma, I'm Dancin,'* and enough

[1] In November of 1950, however, Harold danced his first - and only - Balanchine premiere with the New York City Ballet - the *Mazurka* from *A Life For The Tsar*.

was probably enough.[1]

So Harold danced only in a few ballets by Balanchine (*Symphony in C, Bourree Fantastique*) and one by Lew Christensen (*Jinx*), but to little acclaim. Balanchine's ballets always primarily showcased the ballerina at the expense of the danseur, and Harold's size limited his ability to partner NYCB's famous stable of long-legged beauties. (Others would compare his ballerinas to a bouquet of long-stemmed American-red roses.) Balanchine's adoration of the female was a recognized fact. As Beatrice Gottlieb wrote in the October 1951 issue of Theatre Arts:

So much is given to the enhancement of the female form that, again as in fashion magazines, men fade out of sight...In Balanchine's work, the love duet may be the formal basis, but the actual basis is the glorification of female beauty. The male is put in a position of tertiary importance, less importance, that is, than the female corps de ballet. There are few strong male dancers in Balanchine's company; and what he usually gives men to do is meaningless.

Harold would probably been better off staying in New York.

The tour began successfully, but eventually sputtered out during a London heat wave that turned the unairconditioned theaters into steam baths. A short regional tour was no better; the company finally gave up and came home in the red. That experience reminded him that musical theatre not only showed his talents off in a better light, it also paid better. From then on he would appear only occasionally as a "guest artist" in ballet.

---

[1] I want to note this was never directly conveyed to me by Harold. In his later years it was always interesting to notice what Harold *didn't* say about his ex-comrades with the brilliant and lasting theater careers that had eluded him; like Leonard Bernstein, Jerome Robbins and Bob Fosse. One always got the feeling that he was being careful what he said; someday they might still come to him with a new show.

BOURREE FANTASQUE

CLASSICAL BALLET

Music by Emmanuel Chabrier*
Choreography by George Balanchine
Costumes designed and executed by Barbara Karinska
Lighting by Jean Rosenthal

The first section of *Bourree Fantasque*, using the music of the title piece, is an ironic comment on stage elegance ; the second section to music from Chabrier's opera *Gwendolyn*, is a lyric interlude ; the third, the Fête Polonaise from his opera *Le Roi Malgre Lui*, is a festive finale. The ballet was first presented by the New York City Ballet in October, 1949.

BOURREE FANTASQUE

TANAQUIL LECLERCQ   HAROLD LANG

BARBARA BOCHER, DORIS BRECKENRIDGE, VIDA BROWN, JILLANA, UNA KAI,

RUTH SOBOTKA, BARBARA WALCZAK, TOMI WORTHAM

and

DICK BEARD, BROOKS JACKSON, SHAUN O'BRIEN, ROY TOBIAS

Bourree Fantasque   **New York City Ballet**   **August 2, 1950**

Harold partners the beautiful Tanaquil LeClercq, who would become Balanchine's third ballerina wife two years later. (Sadly, "Tanny" would be stricken with polio while on tour in 1956 and would never dance again.)

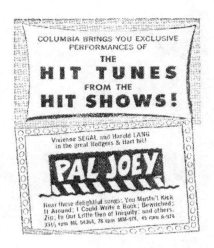

Recording Pal Joey - September 21, 1950

When Harold returned from the NYCB tour, he was scheduled for a recording session. An album of songs from *Pal Joey* for Columbia Records was being recorded at the CBS 30th Street Studios. It had been ten years since the show closed on Broadway, but "cast albums" hadn't been made in 1940. The original female lead, Vivenne Segal, was available to sing her songs, but the original male lead, Gene Kelly, was busy in Hollywood. Besides, while ten years had little effect on the "older woman" role, it might have been more of a problem for a man trying to recapture Joey's youthful enthusiasm for life. Harold's voice had improved, and it fitted the style of Rodgers and Hart score; such a sexy and cynical baritone that even a love song was a come-on.

The record became a big hit, and his first successful venture that didn't involve dancing. Harold couldn't help hoping it would lead to landing the "Joey" role in the revival he was sure would come. The original show had been ahead of its time, but the 1950s was ready for sex and sin.

In the meantime, he needed a job. Nanette Fabray was going to star in a new musical, *Make A Wish*, and, while it didn't look entirely promising from the outset, it had a good part for a singer/dancer. And it would also reunite him with his favorite partner, Helen Gallagher.

Make A Wish was based on the well-loved Ferenc Molnar play, "The Good Fairy," in which a French orphan escapes her lonely life to find love and glamour in the chorus line of a Parisian nightclub. Fabray played the orphan, Janette. Melville Cooper played a wealthy patron and Stephen Douglas played a young law student, both in love with the glamorous Janette. Harold played an American tourist who was interested in a Paris lovely (Helen Gallagher). There were great dance numbers ("The Sale," "The Student's Ball") and gorgeous scenery ("For some reason or other," Brooks Atkinson wrote, "there does seem to be more scenery than show"), but neither the script or the score was equal to the talents of the cast. To everyone's disappointment -- especially Fabray, who personally loved the score -- it closed after only 102 performances.

Harold didn't lose anything for doing the show. He and Helen had "ample time to prove themselves the most winning and versatile singing and dancing team at the moment," according to Atkinson. TIME noted, "Harold Lang and Helen Gallagher are an expert dance team, who have bounce without brashness, know how to handle a song."

Occasionally they had been teaming up for nightclubs and television shows in a half-professional/half-romantic relationship that would last for years. In October of 1951 they sang and danced "On the Boardwalk of Atlantic City" for the Jackie Gleason Comedy Hour, and Helen would remember how they followed a Gleason comedy skit that featured a can of talcum powder. This being live television, there was no time to clean the stage, and suddenly Helen and Harold - who had rehearsed earlier on a spotless stage - found themselves "slipping and sliding" through the number. Watching the kinescope of the performance today, no one would have been the wiser.

As always, they were perfect together.

Nannette Fabray

Harold Lang, Nannette Fabray, Helen Gallagher

Stephen Douglass, Nanette Fabray, Harold and Helen Gallagher

Winter Garden

THE · PLAYBILL · A · WEEKLY · PUBLICATION · OF · PLAYBILL · INCORPORATED

Week beginning Monday, April 23, 1951   Matinees Wednesday and Saturday

HARRY RIGBY and JULE STYNE
with ALEXANDER H. COHEN
Present

NANETTE FABRAY

In a New Musical Comedy

MAKE A WISH

Book by PRESTON STURGES
Music and Lyrics by HUGH MARTIN
Based on "The Good Fairy" by FERENC MOLNAR
Dances and Musical Ensembles by GOWER CHAMPION
Settings and Costumes by RAOUL PENE DU BOIS

Featuring

STEPHEN DOUGLASS   HELEN GALLAGHER   PHIL LEEDS
MARY FINNEY   SYLVIA MANON TRIO   EDA HEINEMANN

With

HAROLD LANG

And

MELVILLE COOPER

Musical Direction by   Vocal Arrangements by   Orchestrations by
MILTON ROSENSTOCK   MR. MARTIN   PHIL LANG · ALLAN SMALL

Vocal Direction by   Dance Music Arranged by
BUSTER DAVIS   RICHARD PRIBOR

ENTIRE PRODUCTION STAGED BY JOHN C. WILSON

HAROLD LANG (Richard Jones)

Harold Lang was the dancing Bill Calhoun in "Kiss Me, Kate," a role he quit to tour England with the New York City Ballet. Born in San Francisco, he found experience and later eminence with the Ballet Russe de Monte Carlo and the Ballet Theatre. His first encounter with the Broadway theatre was "Mr. Strauss Goes to Boston," which he is now able to excuse as a mistake of youth. Thenceforward he chose more cautiously and with better luck. He was one of the three sailors in the Ballet Theatre's "Fancy Free," later expanded into "On the Town." He scored a success in "Three To Make Ready," no easy trick since the star, Ray Bolger, is something of a dancer himself. A leading role with Nancy Walker in "Look, Ma, I'm Dancing" (which had a Hugh Martin score) brought him to the doorstep of "Kiss Me, Kate."

Playbill title page and bio

THEATER

IN A NIFTY PIN-STRIPE SUIT, HAROLD LANG, AS PAL JOEY, WEARS BLASE SMIRK WHICH MARKS HIM AS A LADY-KILLER AND AN ALL-AROUND HOT NUMBER

THE HEEL AS A HERO

In 11 years public gets used to the idea and welcomes him back to Broadway in a revival of 'Pal Joey'

Joey, the all-American heel, who boosted his income as a Chicago hoofer by mooching off women, was first exposed to Broadway as the hero of a musical, *Pal Joey*, in 1940. Though the show made a star out of Gene Kelly it lost money. But ever since then Broadway connoisseurs have claimed that *Pal Joey*, which was based on a series of John O'Hara stories, was ahead of its time in the musical field because it

had a real plot and unconventional characters.

This month the public, and some of the critics, who 11 years ago refused to accept the heel-hero, decided he was both funny and fascinating. They welcomed *Pal Joey* back, and the show is now a roaring success. From the original cast it still has sunny Vivienne Segal as rich Mrs. Simpson, who scoops up Joey from his nightclub and appropriates him for her own

pleasures. It has Harold Lang—a fine dancer—as Joey, who succumbs to Mrs. Simpson and then loses her because he stupidly falls prey to blackmail. It has the best hoofing chorus Broadway has seen in years, and a dozen of Rodgers' and Hart's most exuberant songs including *Bewitched, Bothered and Bewildered*. On a more sophisticated level, *Pal Joey* may turn out to be as much of a Broadway classic as *Showboat*.

CONTINUED ON NEXT PAGE 67

Ad in the December 21, 1951 New York Times:

SEATS TOMORROW AT BOX OFFICE
Mail orders filled promptly
Opens Thurs. Eve., Jan 3
"PAL JOEY"

****

In 1940 the original production of *Pal Joey* had been one of those rare Broadway "Success/Failure" stories, resulting in the often-quoted line from Brooks Atkinson's review, "...can you draw sweet water from a foul well?" It was ahead of its time in many ways, not the least of which was the score by Richard Rodgers and Lorenz Hart. But it also had a risqué story line that shocked the World War II audiences looking for innocent fun and happy endings.

Pal Joey was... well, *dirty*. Rich older woman keeps young stud on a financial leash, trying to keep his sexual charms to herself. He tries to balance launching a dance career with seducing as many girls as possible. A show like this was the complete opposite of a Rogers-Hammerstein classic that would become the smash hit only a few years later, *Oklahoma!* Joey is a heel, but his immaturity keeps the audience from despising him; everyone is kept hoping that someday meeting "the right woman" will bring out his true, decent character.

It doesn't.

NEW YORK TIMES, December 30, 1951

Pal Joey: History Of A Heel   *by Richard Rodgers*

Larry Hart loved PAL JOEY not only because it was successful and people said good things about his work in it, but because of Joey, himself. Joey is a disreputable character, and Larry understood and liked disreputable characters. He knew what John O'Hara knew -- that Joey was not disreputable because he was mean, but because he had too much imagination to behave himself, and because he was a little weak. If you don't understand this about Joey, you'll probably find him hard to take. If you do understand it, you'll be able to chuckle at him and understand him in more than a superficial sense.

Joey as a person met with a great deal of resistance in 1940 when he was first presented to the American public, but I have an idea that this was due largely to the fact that nobody like Joey had ever been on the musical stage before. In the conventional sense, his characteristics were those of a villain, and so long as there was an orchestra in the pit, the villain was supposed to wear a black mustache and be nasty all the way. Since that time, however, characters in musical plays have become more human, and the attitude of the public toward these characters has become more human, too.

While Joey himself may have been fairly adolescent in his thinking and his morality, the show bearing his name certainly wore long pants, and in many respects forced the entire musical comedy theater to wear long pants for the first time. We were all pretty proud of this fact.

****

By 1951, however, partially thanks to Dr. Kinsey, the country had developed a taste for the sleazier side of life. The magnificent score by Rodgers and Hart had never gone out of style, and the recording by Vivienne Segal and the young song-and-dance man from *Kiss Me, Kate* became a smash hit. Why not remount the entire production; using Harold Lang as a "temporary" male lead until a "bigger name" could be lured into the cast? Gene Kelly was in Hollywood, but surely there were other Broadway stars who would sell their soul to play Joey. Harold would later tell how he was given the lead and rehearsals started, but somehow his contract kept getting held up in "negotiations" while the producers busied themselves trying to interest more bankable stars. Fortunately, when Vivienne Segal realized what was happening she went right to her dear friend, Harold, and together they launched a counter-campaign by locking themselves in their dressing rooms until a formal contract was slipped under his door. Harold finally had the part that would define his career, and his partner Helen Gallagher would also have one of her best roles.[1]

Opening night couldn't have been better. In the new Brooks Atkinson review, this production was "brilliant." And what did he have to say about Harold?

It would be hard to improve upon Harold Lang's performance as the heel of Chicago night life. He acts with the cheap guile that Mr. O'Hara caught in his pitiless portrait of one of the most revolting characters in current letters -- plausible, clever, superficially ingratiating, but consistently odious when the balance is struck.

Mr. Lang is pleasant as a singer. As a dancer he is superb; he is light, swift, gay and inventive. If there was ever any doubt about the genuineness of his talent, Mr. Lang has removed it with this searching and resourceful performance.

But then the formidable Brooks Atkinson had always been kind to Harold, something few performers could claim. Atkinson was, as Hume Cronyn put it, "a damn fine critic -- there are few like that around,"[2] but his word on Broadway was the equivalent of an emperor's thumb's up or down in the Roman Coliseum.

There was no doubt about it now, Harold was truly a star. A *big* star.

****

[1] Interestingly enough, when Gallagher left the cast in December 1952, she was succeeded by another of Harold's ex-girlfriends, Nancy Walker.
   [2] *On Broadway*, pg. 324.

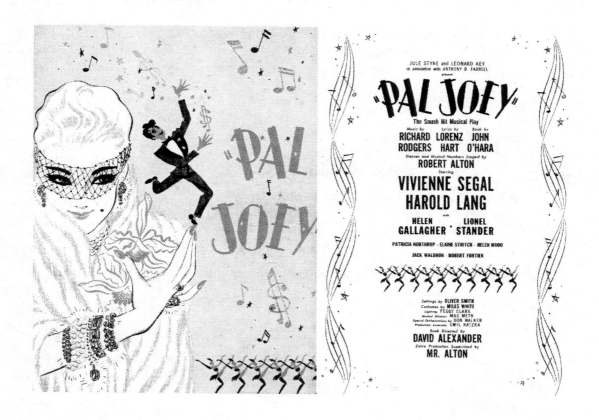

MISS SEGAL was Vera in the original production of "Pal Joey," and so completely did she make the role her own that there never was any question about who would play Joey's benefactress this time around. Born in Philadelphia, Miss Segal began her Broadway career at the top in her first New York appearance; she played the leading role in "Blue Paradise." Other musical comedies followed: "The Clinging Vine," "Adrienne," "Riguette," "Castles in the Air," "The Little Whopper," "Oh Lady, Lady!" and a number of Ziegfeld Follies. She set the Riffs swooning in "The Desert Song" and was D'Artagnan's Constance in "The Three Musketeers," then went out to Hollywood to make such pictures as "The Cat and the Fiddle," "Song of the West," "Bride of the Regiment," "Viennese Nights" and "Golden Dawn." It was the late Lorenz Hart who rescued her from lotus land. Although she had made her reputation as an ingenue, Hart wanted her to play a cynical Countess in "I Married an Angel." He knew there was a great tough comedienne buried beneath the ruffles, so he'd seen her play Peaches in a California production of "Louie in the Air." In "I Married an Angel" Miss Segal called through the naughty measures of "A Twinkle in Your Eye" as if she anward them, and Broadway had a new comedy star. "Pal Joey" came along a couple of seasons later, with Miss Segal triumphantly authoritative as Vera, and Gene Kelly off on his way to stardom as Joey. Miss Segal played Queen Morgan Le Fay in the revival of Rodgers and Hart's "A Connecticut Yankee," and was last seen in "Great to Be Alive." In private life she is Mrs. Hubbell Robinson, her Robinson being a vice-president of a major radio network.

MR. LANG last appeared on Broadway in "Make A Wish" the season before. he lent exuberance and wit to one of the principal roles in "Kiss Kate." A native of California, Mr. Lang had his early dance training at the Opera Ballet School in San Francisco, then went far afield to Logan, Utah, to make his professional debut at the Kling in Massine's ballet "Blue Danube." The San Francisco Opera Ballet Company spotted him and sent him out on tour as a soloist. Mr. Lang subsequently toured with the Ballet Russe de Monte Carlo and Ballet Theatre, and then joined his first musical comedy, "Mr. Strauss Goes To Boston." That wartime occupied him but briefly, and the show spent a season with a stock company in Shamford, Conn., playing juvenile leads in "Over 21," "Boy Meets Girl" and "The Spider." This lyric stage beckoned him back for "Three To Make Ready"; Ray Bolger was starred, and Mr. Lang was a leading dancer. A few seasons ago he played the romantic lead in "Look, Ma, I'm Dancing," and later went on to the above-mentioned "Kiss Me, Kate" and "Make A Wish." Supper club patrons knew him for his work at the Wedgewood Room of the Waldorf-Astoria, the Thunderbird in Las Vegas and the Mocambo in Hollywood. It was Richard Rodgers, composer of "Pal Joey's" score, who suggested him for his present role.

from original 1952 souvenir program

- 64 -

Joey Looks Into The Future

In *The Rise and Fall of the Broadway Musical* Mark N. Grant calls Robert Alton's 'Joey Looks Into the Future,' "arguably the first character-driven dream ballet."

(left)
The hometown boy takes his friends out to Chinatown for dinner after a 1953 San Francisco performance of *Pal Joey*.

(l to r)
unidentified restaurant owner, Neil Hartley (production stage manager), Carol Bruce and Harold Lang

IN THE NIGHTCLUB where Pal Joey works, a team with delusions of sexiness does a dance—and is hilariously parodied by Helen Gallagher and Robert Fortier.

AFTER THE SHOW, Joey is visited by rich dowager, Mrs. Simpson (Segal). Though he has insulted her on a previous meeting, she is smitten

LIFE magazine January 12, 1952

The show ran over a year on Broadway; 542 performances to be exact. And Harold showed up for every one of them. Why? Naturally, he craved the hit starring role he'd always dreamed about, but there was another reason. Waiting in the wings was an eager understudy named Bob Fosse, who had starred in a successful summer stock production of the show and had thought for one brief moment the Broadway role was going to be his. Instead, he cooled his heels backstage waiting for Harold to break an ankle, show up drunk, or better yet - not show up! It never happened, and Fosse had to wait ten years to play the role in a New York City Center revival production.[1] (In the meantime, he also had to make do with becoming one of the most famous direct/choreographers in history.)

Pal Joey - 1953 National Tour

Pal Joey closed on Broadway only to begin all over again as a first-class touring production that would run nearly as long as the original. For a year it toured the country; Chicago, Seattle, Los Angeles, Washington, DC; by all standards a successful tour with a great cast. Vivienne Segal had been replaced by Carol Bruce just before the show closed, and the role had landed in good hands. Carol had a smoky, soulful voice that had won raves in the 1946 revival of *Showboat* when she sang "Bill." She and Harold were able to pull off the same on-stage chemistry that he and Vivienne had. Joey and Vera have to both be rather lousy human beings, but the audience has to believe they're attracted to each other for that very reason. Who's worse? The gigolo, or the woman who's willing to pay for his services?

[1] Ever the gentleman, Harold showed up for Bob's opening night. (With Helen Gallagher as his date.)

In a 2001 interview in her Hollywood apartment, Carol Bruce would tell me:

I only played the New York company after Vivienne Segal left, so for about three weeks I was "breaking in" playing Vera, and that's when I met Harold. I didn't have any real impression that day. He was very sweet, he was very kind, you know -- with a great smile, dancing eyes and all that kind of thing. And I think he was impressed, from the beginning, with me. I think it was an instant kind of rapport that we had right along. I loved it when in the show I would always call him "B-e-a-u-t-y" whenever I wanted him at my feet, or in my bed – "B-e-a-u-t-y!!!"

We started off on tour quite quickly, after about three weeks in New York so I could always say I did do "Pal Joey" on Broadway -- a very short run! But then all that wonderful year, finally ending up in San Francisco. In Chicago we had quite a run; I think months and months. I remember we all stayed at the Ambassador East -- no, no, West, sorry. The West was the one you stayed at! And we'd go up on the roof because it was summertime and all -- I'd always be up there getting a small suntan, not too much, but just enough! But I'd always be up there with rollers in my hair for the show that night. Harold would come up and say, "Oh, there she is -- Dolly Madison." I loved that. I would crack up, "All right! That's quite enough, thank you!" He had everyone else calling me "Dolly."

Anyway, we had a wonderful run in Chicago and the two of us would scoot right next door to the "watering hole" after the show. We were always drinking a lot of "water!" Good name for it -- "water," right? But we had laughs and we were there after the show until about two o'clock in the morning. I think I'd help him home and someone else helped me home and so forth, but we were always on that stage and on time. Never showing up "under the influence" - never! That's one thing I'm very conscientious about, because I had a problem. I didn't recognize it until years later that I was abusing alcohol, and I no longer have -- for 25 years, thus far.

But at any rate, Harold and I - we had laughs, you know. We got to San Francisco and had a wonderful time there! I'll never forget – we were going to the races one day and-- I can not believe this but it's true – they had a horse running, "Pal Joey," right? And I said, "That's ridiculous. I suppose you're all going to bet on 'Pal Joey' and he's going to be limping along." So I'm the only one who didn't bet on "Pal Joey" – everybody cleaned up. It won! It won and Harold said, "Nah, nah, nah!" He cracked up!! You know, I cried all the way home.

But then we were always out pretty much together after the show. As I've said, it was a warm, warm relationship; we never had an unpleasant moment on stage – never! I remember him many times for his great ballet at the end of the first act. I would be enthralled. I could not believe what this man was doing on the stage. And I would think back to the two of us the night before – not in total possession of our faculties! Many times we got him to bed. But never the less, you know, a pro is a pro. To see him! The turns and the elevation and so forth and so on, right down to the apron of the stage, and I would think, "Lord bless him."

I also remember when we got to London for the show and we were still in rehearsal, we were out with Jack[1] to see a show -- I forgot whether it was at the Palladium, but we're walking together and all of a sudden we hear a round of applause. Both of us started to bow to the audience, you know – sort of acknowledge the applause? And then he said, "It's not for us, Carol!" There was someone right in front of us walking to his seat who was one of England's favorite comics – at this moment I've forgotten his name, but he was a star. He had preceded us and he was acknowledging it but the two of us were bowing! And then [Harold] said a word that – well, I shouldn't use it, not on this tape, anyway but it wasn't terribly complimentary to me, "Stop bowing, you 'who-what' – it's not for us!" and the two of us slunk into our seats. But we were hysterical because, God bless, a ham is a ham! We heard applause and we bowed.

It was nice because our dressing rooms were adjacent in the theater and there was always laughs in between. In London we did a "Twilight Matinee," two shows back to back, you see? Two o'clock in the afternoon – five or six and then we got out of the theater early. But in between shows, because they were back to back, I used to make a health drink for both of us. I had the blender and I threw in orange juice and egg and all that good stuff. And [Harold] said, "Oh, you got that -- 'S, H'--- cooking again!" I said, "Yeah, come on – ready!" You know, that's all we had time for because you really didn't feel like eating. But I rather liked the idea because two shows like that back to back, you really didn't get that tired. You were still revved up and it was kind of wonderful. In New York when I did a show it was a two o'clock matinee and then eight-thirty curtain and, yes, you had a chance for dinner, but you fell apart a little bit. I used to have to nap in my dressing room. I'd have a good nap before I could go on at night, and occasionally have a "pick 'em up" pill, what was it? Deximil or something? Yeah, Deximil, to give you some energy for the night time. But over there I had our blended drink and that did it. And we went on and boom – got finished. Many times he'd go his way, because I was having a little "do" with a gentleman who owned one of the finest nightclubs in London. And so I went my private way and he went his way. Sometimes we did something together; sometimes he joined us over there, but we both had a ball. Had a ball!

One particular night I do remember, I had some very unpleasant news from home, and it made me very sad. I couldn't get my make-up on and we had to get on in a very short time. My little beloved, English dresser, Ethel, who was not even five feet tall, very tiny -- she used to have to stand on a box to zip me up! Ethel, who was so Cockney, would pat me on the shoulder and say, "There, there, dearie; don't tyke on so. These things are meant to try us." Try us – I never forgot that! Then Harold came in and said, "Ah, honey – shut up and put your make-up on!" That was it, you know.

---

[1]Jack Hilton, the London producer

He left the company in London. Well, he'd been with a long run on Broadway, on the road in America and then over in London, and he was very tired. Very. I was heartsick to see him go, that I can tell you. And a very nice young man, Dick Francis, took that part and he was very good. He wasn't Harold, but he was very good. And that's it. I just remember being heartsick that he was leaving because we'd been together so long.

****

When they'd played San Francisco, Harold performed the "home-town boy made good" role to the hilt. He posed for photos with the wife of the Opera House manager who had known him from his early ballet days, entertained fellow cast members at the best Chinatown restaurants, and made the obligatory "trip home" to Daly City where hordes of family members crammed themselves into his family's tiny house for a victory celebration. As brother Al would later remember it, there were aunts, uncles and cousins sitting and eating his mom's Mexican food all the way out to the sidewalk; "at least sixty people." Al and Harold's mother, of course, saw the show from the best seats in the house and met the cast afterward. The part Harold was playing may have been "a heel", but it was a heterosexual heel -- a far cry from seeing their boy in tights, dancing in a ballet company. "Joey" was a character they could enjoy, and – according to the local critics -- Harold's performance was never better.[1]

****

---

[1] In one San Francisco interview he claimed he was only 29, an amazingly four-years younger than those who had gone through school with him in Daly City! But it made a better story if "Joey" was under thirty, and did he care what the kids who snubbed him at Jefferson High School thought? When his old principal and several classmates visited him after a performance and proposed a "Harold Lang Day" at the school, Harold enthusiastically accepted -- and then, true to form, never bothered to show up for the festivities.

110

That young Harold Lang, N'York's newest darlin' as the star of the revived musical, "Pal Joey," is a San Franciscan; went through school here, and graduated to B'way via the S. F. Ballet.

Returning as Star Is Thrill for Harold Lang

By Hortense Morton
Drama Editor, The Examiner

"LOCAL BOY makes good" stories are as plentiful around a drama editor's desk as are ashes around her fireplace. Generally, the former have the same nuisance value as the latter.

And, generally, the local kid has only a long distance nodding acquaintance with the assistant, assistant director . . . isn't mentioned in the cast . . . or was eating at a counter hash palace while Marilyn Monroe was dining two blocks away.

But relatives and friends, full of fondness, send in squibs or make detailed phone calls (always at deadline time). Sincerely I can't quarrel with this loyalty; is a sound institution. Sometimes I wish kinfolk and old school mates would realize that there are smart press agents, employed at salaries you

and I don't believe, who take care of the actors—who deserve a reader once.

"Pal Joey," due September 15 at the Geary, brought this to mind . . . all because one Harold Lang, born in Daly City, is masculine star of the Rodgers-Hart-O'Hara hit. The bigger they are, the less outside interference . . . In Lang's case but nothing! When you are at the top, you don't need help, and even the most doting friend wouldn't dare to trespass.

In a long distance interview with Lang this week at the Bev-

Harold Lang, the former San Francisco the star of "Pal Joey"

'Pal Joey' Star Glad to Get Home

(Continued from Page 10)

erly-Wilshire Hotel where the company of "Pal Joey" had just checked in from Chicago, we got the pitch.

"I've been talking California for weeks," admitted Lang. "The company has bought every copy of "Holiday" with that article about San Francisco. They are pouring over it. I'm a heel. Compulsory reading. But, it's wonderful coming back as the star of a production. It's wonderful being able to introduce my home town to a lot of people who have never been there. I can hardly wait to see their faces."

THE GOOD FEELING

We know how it feels. We've gone into this before. But, every morning when I tool down Portola Drive from my home on Teresita Boulevard, I got a big pitch when I see cars with out-of-state license plates and their owners taking pictures of San Francisco from Observation Point. Love those smart tourists and wish that I could again see San Francisco for the first time.

Lang, whom I've never met, seemed like a very nice boy over the phone. What am I saying, "boy"! He's 29. Remember the remark of Oscar Wilde "after you reach a certain age, all policemen seem younger than

you." I've reached a certain age, one deserving of respect, but traffic police passing out citations never seem to respect grey hairs.

SHOW BUSINESS URGE

Phone interviews are rugged. You miss the personal approach but you do get detailed facts. The warm personality. The sincere voice. That's Lang, the lad whose mother lives in Daly City and who says:

"I'm bringing her into town and to the St. Francis Hotel when we open at the Geary. I'll have to do a lot of rehearsing, interviews, radio, TV, etc., but if she's 'down home' I won't get to see much of her. This way, we can lunch together and she can go with me on many of the interviews."

Part Spanish and part French, his great-great grandfather was third mayor (or Alcade) of San Francisco. His name was Martinez. Lang isn't too sure. He went to Woodrow Wilson and Vista Grande Schools and graduated from Jefferson Union High. As a Western Union messenger, serving the Russ Building, he got his first taste of show business when he delivered a telegram to a ballerina backstage at the San Francisco Opera House. Also, he sang in the choir at Grace Cathedral. That Opera House delivery

gave him the urge to dance. Came enrollment in the Christensen Brothers Ballet. Then New York and "Fancy Free." You figure it out from there. Success.

First wishers will welcome home San Franc

London release of *Pal Joey* cast recording, featuring
"HAROLD LANG and a Brilliant American Cast"

Pal Joey - London, 1954

The national tour was over and the company barely had time to catch their collective breaths when the opportunity came to do a London production. Carol Bruce said "Yes!" with joy and not a minute's hesitation, but Harold was a harder sell. He'd been "Joey" for nearly three years and for someone whose interest in a job lasted for a few months at most, that was an eternity. However, when nothing else definite was offered, he accepted -- but for a brief run only. Although the springtime London reviews were excellent, by late 1954 Dick Francis had taken over the role and Harold was back in New York, his real "hometown," rehearsing for an off-Broadway revival production, *Time of Your Life*.

He didn't realize it then, but the time of his life was just about over.

January 16, 1955
Hirschfeld cartoon,

Time of Your Life

Some loungers in Nick's waterfront saloon, the setting for "The Time of Your Life." Franchot Tone is in the foreground. Harold Lang is dancing and Myron McCormick, as Nick, serves Gloria Vanderbilt. The revival opens at the City Center Wednesday night.

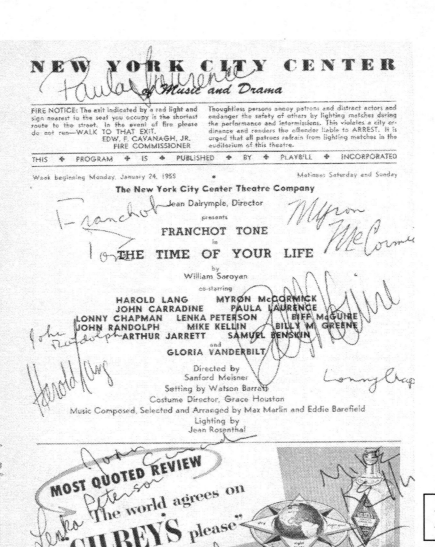

NEW YORK CITY CENTER
of Music and Drama

FIRE NOTICE: The exit indicated by a red light and sign nearest to the seat you occupy is the shortest route to the street. In the event of fire please do not run—WALK TO THAT EXIT.
EDW. F. CAVANAGH, JR.
FIRE COMMISSIONER

Thoughtless persons annoy patrons and distract actors and endanger the safety of others by lighting matches during the performance and intermissions. This violates a city ordinance and renders the offender liable to ARREST. It is urged that all patrons refrain from lighting matches in the auditorium of this theatre.

THIS ✦ PROGRAM ✦ IS ✦ PUBLISHED ✦ BY PLAYBILL ✦ INCORPORATED

Week beginning Monday, January 24, 1955 • Matinees Saturday and Sunday

The New York City Center Theatre Company

Jean Dalrymple, Director

presents

FRANCHOT TONE
in
THE TIME OF YOUR LIFE

by
William Saroyan

co-starring

HAROLD LANG	MYRON McCORMICK
JOHN CARRADINE	PAULA LAURENCE
LONNY CHAPMAN	LENKA PETERSON	BIFF McGUIRE
JOHN RANDOLPH	MIKE KELLIN	BILLY M. GREENE
ARTHUR JARRETT	SAMUEL BENSKIN

and

GLORIA VANDERBILT

Directed by
Sanford Meisner
Setting by Watson Barratt
Costume Director, Grace Houston
Music Composed, Selected and Arranged by Max Marlin and Eddie Barefield
Lighting by
Jean Rosenthal

MOST QUOTED REVIEW
"The world agrees on
GILBEY'S please"

Gilbey's Distilled London Dry Gin, 90 Proof, 100% Grain Neutral Spirits, W. & A. Gilbey, Ltd.

Autographed *Playbill* title page

THE TIME OF YOUR LIFE

January 18, 1955

New York City Center Theatre Company (Jean Dalrymple, director) revival of a play by William Saroyan in two acts; directed by Sanford Meisner, setting by Watson Barratt, lighting by Jean Rosenthal, costume director, Grace Houston; music composed, selected and arranged by Max Marlin and Eddie Barefield.

THE CAST

THE NEWSBOY	Art Ostrin	McCARTHY	John Randolph
JOE	Franchot Tone	NICK'S MA	Rosana San Marco
ARAB	Wolfe Barzell	KIT CARSON	John Carradine
THE DRUNKARD	Billy M. Greene	SAILOR	Tom Erasmus
NICK	Myron McCormick	ANNA	Lenka Berlin
WILLIE	Fred Korman	ELSIE	Gloria Vanderbilt
TOM	Lonny Chapman	A STREETWALKER	Betty Eartley
KITTY DUVAL	Lenka Peterson	HER SIDE-KICK	Doris Roberts
HARRY	Harold Lang	A SOCIETY LADY	Paula Laurence
DUDLEY	Biff McGuire	A SOCIETY GENTLEMAN	Albert Whitley
WESLEY	Samuel Benskin	FIRST COP	Clifton James
LORENE	Justine Johnston	SECOND COP	John Pellatt
BLICK	Arthur Jarrett	OTHERS	David Martin
MARY L.	Carol Grace		Nina Wilcox
KRUPP	Mike Kellin		

Company manager, Gilman Haskell; production stage manager, Buford Armitage, stage managers, Herman Shapiro and Edwin Gifford, press representative, Tom Trenkle.

Franchot Tone played the role of Joe, the barroom philosopher with a penchant for collecting odd items, and not reading newspapers, in the revival of The Time of Your Life.

THEATRE ARTS, APRIL, 1955

Theatre Arts April 1955

- 74 -

CHAPTER 5: 1955-57
SLIPPERY SLOPE

Time Of Your Life - January 1955

It wasn't a starring role, but it had *class*, theater prestige. The City Center was reviving *The Time of Your Life*, a 1939 modern classic by William Saroyan that took place in a San Francisco bar.[1]

It was a good part in a good show, but only for a limited run. Even with the best reviews it could only serve to remind people that Harold Lang was still around. Perhaps the best thing to come out of it for Harold was a delightful Al Hirschfeld cartoon in the January 16, 1955 New York Times showing "Harry the Hoofer" dancing under the amused gaze of Franchot Tone, the show's star. No, it wasn't the follow-up to *Pal Joey* he'd wanted. And there wasn't much else waiting when it was over.

This wasn't the way it was supposed to work. He had been a smash on Broadway; won three Donaldson awards (from *Billboard* magazine) as "Best Dancer on Broadway," now Hollywood was supposed to come calling, like they had for Kelly and Astaire, and even for his old Ballet Theatre buddy Tommy Rall. So why didn't they? Harold was always very elusive on that point, making it sound like moviemaking was a bore and he was more excited by live audiences. He said he'd visited a bunch of friends on the set of *Seven Brides For Seven Brothers* and they all told him how lucky he was not to be mixed up in such a tedious, frustrating process. (Probably sparing his feelings, knowing Harold would have sold what was left of his soul to be in that hit film.) My opinion, from watching kinescopes of Harold's television work, is that for some reason the moving

---

[1] As if this wasn't enough to make it familiar ground for Harold, the character of Harry, an aspiring tap dancer, had originally been played by Gene Kelly.

camera didn't photograph him well. This sounds puzzling, considering he was at his best *moving*, but the cameras are seeing something besides a dancer; they are catching a personality. Harold's brash, boyish charm might come across the footlights intact, but on the early television stages it came across as tough and sardonic. Instead of an easy smile, he seems to sneer. Suddenly you get an uneasy feeling there is more of the satyr than the kid next door, and 1940s and 50s TV audiences weren't ready to have "Joey Evans" visiting in their living rooms. I think the Hollywood studio head watched the same television shows and thought to themselves that Harold Lang was not film material.

True, the earliest television lighting was crude and the staging was vaudevillian. You were on, you did your "spot" and you were off again, often with little or no rehearsal time in front of a camera. It was "live" TV; what you saw was what you got, and not even a lot of that remains. Probably the easiest piece of film footage to view today was the last (or one of the last), an over-the-top version of "If They Asked Me, I Could Write A Book," staged for a 1954 Ethel Merman-hosted *Shower of Stars* production. In it, Harold impresses a pretty, young schoolteacher, out for a field trip with some of her young students to the zoo. In Joey-esque fashion, Harold bribes the kids to take a powder so he can have his way with the teacher. He throws away her guidebook, sings to her about the kind of book he had in mind, and illustrates it with a lot of monkeying-around, literally. He jumps up on top the cages and dances his imitations of the animals underneath, trying his best to look like Gene Kelly all the time. It's hard to watch the number without thinking he was trying almost too hard for a last-ditch audition. He still had hopes a movie version of *Pal Joey* would be made with the original Broadway cast, something he knew was highly unlikely, given Hollywood's habit of recasting shows using their own contract players. The movie would eventually be made, of course, but not until 1957. The part would be rewritten to make Joey a singer instead of a dancer so Frank Sinatra could play him. And it had a happy ending.

When asked direct questions about his lack of a film career, he was at his most evasive. Finally he said he'd had a screen test once, with Warner Brothers, but it didn't go anywhere. As usually, he couldn't remember the dates. There was a picture of him sitting between Bette Davis and Glenn Ford. Check the film listings for both stars and you find there was only one film they worked on together, *A Stolen Life* in 1946. Look at the picture again and the styles and ages of the people seem about right. Harold looks young and cocky, as if he knows he's on his way up and this is just one more step. He expected the studio that zoomed in on him for a close-up as a waiter in a ballet short to offer him a contract that would put his name on a movie marquee, but it never happened.

inscription from Davis reads: "For Harold - continued success to you. Always, Bette D."
inscription from Ford reads: "To 'Harold' with all my very best wishes - Sincerely, Glenn"

But in the mid-1950s Harold was "at liberty" with no money and no sure prospects. Why else would he pose nude for the notoriously homosexual Vulcan Studio? Probably he thought the photos would be used for "art" collections, sent out to buyers in plain, brown paper wrappers. Did he really look at the photo release contract and realize the studio had the right to sell the pictures to the "muscle men" pulp magazines? In the pre-Stonewall era of closeted gay publications, the physical fitness world provided the only cover for men to see pictures of other naked or half-naked men. Even later, despite years of alcohol abuse Harold's body survived surprisingly well, and perhaps at this point he felt he had nothing else to sell. Always a big spender, buying drinks for the house and living high on his *Joey* salary, he must have been alarmed to find himself as broke as he'd been as a corps de ballet dancer.

So in 1956 anyone who bought a copy of *Trim* or *Body Beautiful* could see artistic poses of Harold Lang in the altogether. The photos were not pornographic. They were tasteful, even classic. No matter. In this "Ozzie and Harriet" period of time, nude photos could end a career. What must the gossip in the performing arts world have been over this, one can only guess. Was he announcing he was homosexual, or broke, or both?

Just when things seems to be on a fast-track downhill, Harold's luck changed again. There was going to be a new musical, and he got of the lead roles.

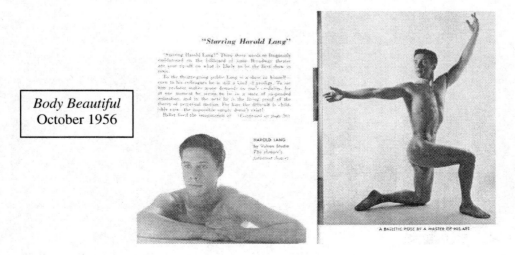

Body Beautiful
October 1956

"*Starring Harold Lang*"

- 78 -

June Holloway and Harold Lang in
Shangri-La

Shangri-La - **June 13, 1956**

It could have been the part that revived his career... if only it had lasted more than 21 performances. He wasn't the "star" (Dennis King had that honor) but *Shangri-La* sounded like a great concept, and for the first time since *Make A Wish* Harold would originate a role instead of playing in a revival production. The part of Robert Henderson, a USO dancer stranded after a plane crash, gave him one of the highlights of the evening - "Talkin' With Your Feet" - but it wasn't enough to save the crashing failure of the show. Opening on a miserably hot New York day with a female lead who had been an emergency replacement for the original star didn't help, but the main reason for the show's demise was the fact there was no magic in a magical story familiar to everyone from the successful film version. Before the end of the summer, Harold was again "at liberty." Meanwhile, his ex-understudy from *Pal Joey*, Bob Fosse was busy choreographing *Bells Are Ringing*, his third hit show in as many years (*Pajama Game, Damn Yankees*). After waiting unsuccessfully through 542 performances for Harold to call in sick, Fosse was now one of Broadway's greatest stars. And there didn't seem to be a part in any of his shows for Harold.

****

Ziegfeld Follies - **March 1, 1957**

A "star turn" in a revue that runs 123 performances on Broadway, for Harold this was the sum total of the year 1957. Even with a big name like Bea Lillie heading the program, musical comedy revues were old hat in a year that would later see the premiere of *West Side Story* (whose female lead, Carol Lawrence, had been in the *Ziegfeld Follies* cast with Harold before landing her breakthrough role.) He did get to do a number from the show on the June 23, 1957 Ed Sullivan Show with Helen Wood, but there was little press coverage, and his name went almost unnoticed.

After the rehearsals, out-of-town premiere and the short New York run of *Ziegfeld Follies*, Harold still had a large part of the year ahead of him with no offers except for a few "nostalgia" record offers (*The Bandwagon* in 1953 and *Jerome Kern Revisited* in 1956) and those he dreaded -- the summer stock shows of small-town America.

HAROLD LANG

Mr. Lang is a prime example of that rare theatrical breed—the dancing star who can truly act and sing. His nimble feet carried him to ballet fame long before he made his musical comedy bow in the short-lived "Mr. Strauss Goes to Boston." Scion of one of the oldest Spanish families in California, Mr. Lang first danced with the San Francisco Opera Ballet, subsequently touring the country with the Monte Carlo Ballet and Ballet Theatre. Following his stage debut, he polished his acting skills playing juvenile leads during a season of stock in Connecticut. He returned to the lyric theatre as lead dancer in "Three To Make Ready", which starred Ray Bolger. His first starring role was in "Look Ma, I'm Dancing", with Nancy Walker, after which he played one of the four principle roles in "Kiss Me, Kate." An appearance in "Make A Wish" preceded his triumphal portrayal of the title role in Rodgers and Hart's "Pal Joey", on Broadway and in London. On the New York stage, he most recently participated in the musicals "Shangri-La" and "Ziegfeld Follies" as well as the off-Broadway revival of "On The Town." He also performed as an actor in "The Time Of Your Life." Between shows, Mr. Lang makes frequent appearances on television and in supper clubs, such as the Wedgewood Room at the Waldorf-Astoria, the Thunderbird in Las Vegas and the Mocambo in Hollywood. He recently completed a co-starring assignment in the National Company of "Once Upon A Mattress."

****

THE PLAYBILL FOR BOSTON

The COLONIAL THEATRE ·

ONCE UPON A MATTRESS

HAROLD LANG
(Jester)

Harold Lang was born in San Francisco, member of the famous Martinez family, holders of one of the original great Spanish Land Grants.

Young Harold earned extra money as a Western Union Messenger. While delivering a telegram to the San Francisco Ballet School, he watched a class, decided dancing looked more interesting than sports, and was soon a ballet student. An audition for famous choreographer Leonide Massine won him a place with the Ballet Russe de Monte Carlo as soloist. After three years with the Ballet Russe he joined the Ballet Theatre, creating many roles including one of the sailors in Jerome Robbins' *Fancy Free*. He appears as guest artist with the New York City Ballet between Broadway shows.

He has starred on Broadway in *Look, Ma, I'm Dancing, Make A Wish, Kiss Me, Kate* and in the revivals of *Pal Joey* and *On the Town*.

Mr. Lang has appeared in TV and summer theatres; and recently returned from a four month tour of England in a revival of *Time of Your Life.*

HAROLD LANG

An outstanding example of that rare theatrical personality, the dancing star who can also sing and act, Harold Lang made a name for himself in ballet long before he took to the musical-comedy stage.

Born in San Francisco, he first danced with the Kosloff Ballet, and then the San Francisco Ballet, where he soon became a leading soloist. Tours with The Ballet Russe de Monte Carlo and with The American Ballet Theatre quickly followed.

His musical-comedy debut was in the short-lived *Mr. Strauss Goes to Boston.* The show folded, but the critics and public sat up and took notice of Harold Lang. Dancing leads in *Three to Make Ready*, starring Ray Bolger, and in *Look, Ma, I'm Dancin!*, with Nancy Walker, led to his success as one of the four stars of Cole Porter's *Kiss Me Kate.*

An appearance in *Make a Wish* preceded his personal triumph as the charming heel in the title role of *Pal Joey* opposite Vivienne Segal. He played the role in New York, London, and on tour.

He has also been seen in *Shangri-La*, in the recent edition of *The Ziegfeld Follies*, in the straight dramatic role of the hoofer in the revival of *The Time of Your Life*, and Off-Broadway in the revival of *On the Town.*

CHAPTER 6: 1958-69

LONG WAY DOWN

On The Town - 1959

As *Ziegfeld Follies* closed, an interesting offer came to Harold; would he like to star in an off-Broadway revival production of *On The Town* at the Carnegie Hall Playhouse? Essentially he would be getting the chance he'd longed for in 1945 -- to take his original "Fancy Free" ballet character into the musical comedy.

Yes, he very much wanted to do that.

Unfortunately, this *On the Town* was a moderate success at best. Maybe it was the "skimpy basement stage" the Playhouse had let them use, or the fact that the review headlines read, "*On The Town* - 14 Years Later." There was another production of the show going on in New York at the same time and perhaps audiences were confused, but the reviews found little new or exciting to comment on except for Pat Carrol's deadpan performance as Hildy. Harold was merely "agreeable" as Gaby. *Agreeable.*

The show ran its allotted time and closed. Harold was again at liberty.

****

A dancer sees himself reflected in the rehearsal hall mirror. Day after day he watches his body sweat, stumble and eventually create magic. The dancer goes onstage and becomes a performer. Seeing himself reflected in the audiences' eyes, in make-up and costume, he watches the magic take hold. His reward is heard in the applause, felt in the love of hundreds of people surging over the footlights until it become an addiction that nothing else can satisfy.

More than anything else Harold dreaded becoming a has-been; one of those pathetic, aging performers repeating the same roles over and over in decreasingly well-known summer stock and regional theatre productions. Unfortunately, by 1959 this is pretty much what had happened. After *On The Town* closed there were no new offers in New York and nothing for him to do but go on the road.

The Dayton, Ohio Theater Festival had him for the summer of 1959, along with Jerry Orhbach. Unlike Harold, Jerry's years of stardom in New York -- first as the original "El Gallo" in *The Fantasticks*, then in *Carnival, Promises, Promises, Chicago*, etc. -- were still ahead of him. With only a successful revival production of *Threepenny Opera* in his resume at this point, sharing the stage with a Broadway veteran like Harold Lang must have been an exciting experience. Together they did productions of *Oklahoma!* and -- of course -- *Pal Joey*. Then Harold was on to North Tonawanda, NY for their Melody Fair; again, *Pal Joey*.

An unexpected opportunity came up in 1959. The original cast recording of *Kiss Me, Kate* -- the first Broadway recording released as a 33 1/3 rpm "long-playing" (LP) 10" record -- was going to be re-recorded in the new, true stereo sound. As an added bonus, the tap-dance that was the real highlight of Harold's solo, "Bianca", would also be recorded this time. On a rainy New York day, Harold brought his dancing shoes to the recording studio only to find no one had told the sound technicians about the need for a wooden dancing floor. The floors of the studio, of course, were carpeted absorb footsteps, not record them. At the last minute, one enterprising technician took the only available wooden door off its hinges and laid it down in front of a microphone for Harold to dance. Unfortunately, it was an outside door that had led into an alleyway, and was therefore soaking wet from the storm. Harold never forgot the misery of tapping out "Bianca" -- a dance he hadn't performed for nearly 20 years -- on a wet door.

Once Upon A Mattress - national touring company: 1960-62

Maybe it was the newly-released recording of *Kiss Me, Kate* that reminded everyone Harold Lang was still around and could still sing, but a lucky break came along in late 1960 when he was offered the part of the "Jester" in a national touring company of *Once Upon A Mattress*, the show that had made Carol Burnett a star in the original Broadway production. It wasn't the lead, but it was a perfect role for Harold's talents. With Hollywood legend Buster Keaton as the "King," the production had class. Harold stayed with the company -- touring St. Louis, Boston, Los Angeles, etc. -- for two years.

In San Francisco he'd have old friends visit, but many of them only wanted to be introduced to Buster Keaton. For Harold, who had been lauded in the same city only seven years ago as "home-town star" in the touring company of *Pal Joey*, appearing as Buster Keaton's jester must had been a bitter pill to swallow. One old buddy had a happier comment on the show, "I didn't really know Harold could sing *that well!*"

****

I Can Get It For You Wholesale - **March 22, 1962**

In his autobiography, *Original Story*, Arthur Laurents tells how Harold showed up to audition for *I Can Get It For You Wholesale*. Nervous, unkempt and smelly, Harold sounds like an aging, alcoholic melodramatic character-- and very possibly he was. Let's remember, too, that Laurents (from his own admission earlier in the book) had been a cast-off lover of Harold's in the 1940's. Certainly, one story from the rehearsal period of Harold dropping his pants backstage comes off as a vindictive little backstab by Laurants. As Nanette Fabray would remark in her own deliciously forthright way -- God bless her -- "Arthur made Harold sound like a *slut!*"

Whatever the truth of the story, Harold did at least end up with an excellent part in a Broadway show, along with a brand-new performer destined to become one of Hollywood's most powerful stars, Barbra Streisand. In fact, the show would be primarily remembered for being "Barbra's debut;" something that always irritated Harold, who didn't get along with the budding diva. Barbra's boyfriend/husband was the young lead of *Wholesale*, Elliot Gould, and their Elizabeth Taylor-Richard Burtonesque fights and lovemaking came to dominate the show's publicity and ruin the cast's backstage camaraderie.

TIME magazine's review on March 30, 1962 said, " Harold Lang and Sheree North (*Bogen's Folly*) make a scorching sex rite out of 'What's In It for Me?" He was back, but for the last time. Although it would run a respectable 300 performances, *Wholesale* wouldn't be enough of a hit to keep Harold on Broadway forver.

Harold, rehearsing with a *very* young (19 years old) Barbra Streisand.

The last Broadway show of his career was behind him, and ahead of him were only more regional theater performances... when he was able to get them. In 1963 he did *Showboat* at Milwaukee's Swan Theatre and *Song of Norway* in Warren, Ohio. Then on to Gaithersburg, Maryland in 1964 for the Shady Grove Music Fair, where he co-starred with Diahann Carroll in *No Strings* and *Little Me*. The newspaper reviews praised Carroll as a "complete actress; a singer both sweet and forceful" and her leading man Walter Farrell as having a "fine voice and easy manner." Then the reviewer damns with faint praise, "Harold Lang does well as Farrell's sidekick." (*Ouch!*)

By 1965 even the summer stock opportunities were drying up with the persistent rumors of Harold's problems onstage. Alcohol was doing to him what it had done to so many other performers. First it had fueled the fire, then it provided the "magic time" when you could relax after a show, now it had become a desperately-needed crutch to deal with the depression of lost stardom. It also dulled the memory and the dancing muscles, making him a liability for any performer sharing the stage with him.

In 1965 a new book by Patrick Dennis ("Auntie Mame") was being published. It followed an imaginary 1900s husband-wife team and their unsavory entourage who briefly take over the highest offices in the country before being carted off to prison. "First Lady" was a spoof on politics and the gullibility of the American electorate, and mock "historical pictures" of the story provided Dennis's friends -- Peggy Cass, Kaye Ballard, Rhonda Fleming, Melissa Hayden and Jacques d'Amboise (appearing as Pavlova and Nijinski, of course), etc. etc. -- with the opportunity to dress in period outfits and pose in a series of outlandish photographs. Kaye Ballard remembers it as a lark inspired by Harold's old buddy, Cris Alexander, the Broadway performer-turner-photographer.

Perhaps hoping the book would be adapted for a musical (as "Auntie Mame" was being adapted for the musical *Mame*) Harold threw himself into the project and was a natural as the drunken, thieving brother-in-law of the President who naturally ends up as Secretary of State. The photos show a convincingly besotted scoundrel whose body (shown in one near-nude shot) was still in excellent, dancer-like condition. The idea might be seen as either a lark with a bunch of wacky, theater friends, but it's a strange collection of pictures, at best. At worst, it was as pathetic a self-exploitation as the body-builder magazine spreads and was never included in his resume. Maybe Harold got a chance to see himself as others saw him when he previewed the prints; drunk, glassy-eyed, leering and laughable.

The book wasn't successful, anyway. It was just another dead end:

TIME Magazine Aug. 7, 1964

FIRST LADY by Martha Dinwiddie Butterfield as told to Patrick Dennis
                                            with photographs by Cris Alexander.

It must have been an absolute giggle of an idea. With the elections coming up and all, it would be a hoot to do a sort of Little Me thing, only about the girl who married the President. All the fun people joined in—Peggy Cass, Dody Goodman, Harold Lang, Dagmar, Kaye Ballard, Jacques d'Amboise, Melissa Hayden, Vicki Cummings and lots of others—and everybody got dressed up in the wildest costumes while Cris Alexander took loads of simply outrageous pictures. Pat's manuscript had everybody in stitches. The joke was a good one when Cecil Beaton produced My Royal Past a generation ago; now, under Dennis' heavier hand, ersatz autobiography-with-snapshots is nothing but a drag.

****

*John Sappington Marmaduke Dinwiddie
("Bubber")*

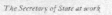

The Secretary of State at work

The Decline And Fall Of The Entire World As Seen Through The Eyes Of Cole Porter Revisited - March 31, 1965

Although "First Lady" never made it to the stage, in 1965 Harold was appearing off-Broadway in a Ben Bagley revue of Cole Porter hits that opened at the Square East Theatre. Although it was a small, informal production it had a stellar cast, and as John S. Wilson of The New York Times wrote in "Theater: Porter's World Revisited,"

> It is quite probable that a highly acclaimed songwriting career could be based entirely on the Cole Porter songs that scarcely anyone but Ben Bagley knows. In any event, Mr. Bagley, an incorrigible collector of forgotten songs from the theater, has built the most tuneful and witty musical in town around what might be considered the unknown Porter.

> He calls it "The Decline and Fall of the Entire World as Seen Through the Eyes of Cole Porter Revisited," a title that all but buries the cast of five performing it on the small stage of the Square East. The "world" under scrutiny is the one that occupied the years between 1929 and 1945, when there can be little doubt that considerable declining and falling went on.

> As Mr. Porter saw these years in his songs, however, it was a period in which an examination of the engagements between the sexes continued to be pertinent. His views of the times were expressed in "How's Your Romance?," "I Loved Him But That Way," "I Loved Him But He Didn't Love Me" and "But in the Morning, No," to mention a few of the full- blooded Porter tunes that might have disappeared with the rest of that world had Mr. Bagley not brought them back to light.

> It is one of the fascinations of this revue that, of its 33 songs, there is not one that rates as a dud; and, barring one chorus of "Let's Do It," one would have to be something of a show-tune buff to be familiar with any of them. They come pouring out of Mr. Bagley's cornucopia, presented with airy abandon by five light-hearted singing and dancing satirists who obviously are in full accord with Mr. Porter's views.

> Kaye Ballard, batting her eyes, baring her gleaming teeth and dodging encircling dancers, is by turns slinky or raucous. She tells the sad story

of an indigestible social-climbing oyster in "Tale of the Oyster," she is Mabel Mercer elegantly declaiming "Down in the Depths on the 90th Floor," Sophie Tucker intoning "Tomorrow" and Beatrice Lillie, stretched out across four stools, and wrapped in a red boa, singing "When I Was a Little Cuckoo."

Carmen Alvarez, an exotic beauty, brings to light a lovely Porter ballad, "What Shall I Do?," takes off her shoes to sing "Find Me a Primitive Man" and, as one of three burlesque queens in "Come On In," mixes bumps with bubble gum. Elmarie Wendel, a versatile pixie; <u>Harold Lang, still handy with both feet and voice</u>, and William Hickey, a man who manages to look studious and baffled at the same time, keep the songs moving...

****

1966-69

By 1967 Harold's photo and bio were still appearing in "Dance World", but the entry had gotten noticeably smaller. Naming the ballet companies he'd danced with, it adds only, "More recently has been seen in musicals." Actually, it would have more honest to say, "Has been seen recently in very little of anything." Harold Lang very nearly drops off the map during this period of time. After dreaming of and finally reaching the Broadway heights, after learning to act like and demanding the privileges of a star, he was broke and scared. Finally he took a job at a men's shop on Times Square. A young dancer from San Francisco recognized him and quickly looked away. "It was so sad," he told me years later, "to see Harold Lang selling shirts."

When did he actually land in California "for good"? Maybe he never really did. Maybe he was just used to coming home for a visit when he had nowhere else to go. Maybe it never occurred to him that he was never going to live in New York City again. As his brother, Al, remembered it, one day in 1970 he got a call from Harold saying, "Al, I'm sick of New York"

"Then come back to California," Al said. And Harold came back.

- 91 -

However, Mike Madill's memories have Harold already beginning a relationship with the fledgling dance department at California State University, Chico as early as 1968, when he accompanied a small group of student performers to the Olympics in Mexico City. Mike promised to send copies of the clippings (they-were-right-in-his-bedroom..), but *mea culpa* - I should have known better. Like Harold, Mike can be charmingly long on promises that he is exasperatingly short on keeping. I tried hiring a research assistant, with dismal results. I should have gone to Chico and searched the newspaper archives myself, but time went by too quickly.

By 1970 Harold was a part of the Chico dance scene, and traveling seventy miles north with Mike and pianist John Vedrine (long-time class accompanist and much loved by the students) to Shasta College for a day of master classes. The Shasta dance director's teaching assistant had broken her foot earlier practicing air turns, and was preparing for class by stretching on the floor with her leg in a cast. Less than a minute after walking in, Harold was squatting on the floor next to her.

What happened?! He really wanted to know. Well, her friends invited her to go skiing last weekend, but she wasn't going to take the chance of breaking her leg just before the ballet master class, so she stayed home like a good girl and practiced instead. When her friends came back from their skiing trip, they found she'd broken her leg coming down wrong out of a *tour en l'air*, and now she'd never live it down.

Was she *still* taking the ballet class with him? Of course she was-- wouldn't miss it for the world. Actually, the hardest part was just getting the tights on over the cast...

He burst out laughing, and the two of us started a conversation that lasted fifteen years.

CHAPTER 7: 1970-84

Safe Haven

Harold had a friend in the business, a casting director named Leonard Finger, who prided himself on giving has-been actors a second chance, often finding parts that no one else would have considered them for. Even Leonard had a point, though, when he felt it was his duty to tell a performer that the fat lady had stopped singing. "There's an old Talmudic saying," he'd remind them, "When three men say you're drunk, lie down."[1] He said that actors had to have a cut-off point when they knew their lives aren't going anywhere, and it's time to move on to something else. This was Harold's time.

For awhile, he stayed with his mother and tried to establish himself as a dance teacher in the Bay Area. Meanwhile, an ex-hoofer from the television show "Your Hit Parade," Mike Madill, had launched an ambitious new degree program for a major in dance at California State University - Chico and needed a ballet instructor. Mike knew Harold from the old days in New York, got the news he was back on the West Coast, and before too long a "guest lecturer" position turned into a teaching job that would last the rest of Harold's life -- by far the longest "run" of his career.

You might be wondering where - and what - is CSU-Chico? First, the city (and this is straight from the Chamber of Commerce):

Located 90 miles north of Sacramento, the City of Chico lies within the northern end of California's lush Sacramento Valley, and is Butte County's largest city. Chico, and

[1]Huetes, Hettie Lynn. *Casting Directors*, pg55

Summer residence until Aug. 31
14 Alp Ave.
Daly City, Calif. 9403

RESUME

HAROLD LANG
Assistant Professor
Department of Physical Education
California State University, Chico
Chico, California   95929

RESIDENCE: Woodoak Apartments #39
555 Vallombrosa
Chico, California 95926
(916)345-3718

PERSONAL AND PROFESSIONAL SUMMARY

Native Californian, scion of one of the earliest California families. Began a professional dancing career with the San Francisco Ballet, then was asked to join the Ballet Russe de Monte Carlo. Extensive U. S. touring with the Ballet Russe. Later was invited to join the American Ballet Theatre. Extensive national and international tours with the latter company, with continuing guest appearances with the American Ballet Theatre - latest, January, 1975, culminating in the gala 35th Anniversary of the American Ballet Theatre's inception. Extensive study with significant ballet dancers and choreographers (for details, see lists of same).

Specializing in dance led to an invitation to perform in musical comedy, which meant broadening professional experiences to singing and acting, also a study of different kinds of dance. Was presented with three Donaldson Awards for the "Best Dancer on Broadway" - 1947, 1948, 1952.

Extensive musical comedy experiences on Broadway, with original New York City companies, and tours that included summer stock productions (performing and directing summer stock), off Broadway shows, etc. (See listing for details.)

Continuing television appearances during this time. Vocal recordings of original cast productions, plus a miscellany of other albums.

Other guest appearances and teaching experiences at the University of Alabama, the Baltimore Actors Theatre, and guest teacher, Ballet Arts, Carnegie Hall, New York City.

Five years of full-time teaching experience at California State University, Chico, teaching ballet, directing and choreographing musicals and dance concerts.

WHAT I WOULD LIKE TO TEACH

I would like to utilize my professional experience to teach the following courses:

BALLET
CHOREOGRAPHY
THEATRICAL REALITIES (Realistic Approaches to Performing Professionally in
the Theatre and Television)
MUSICAL COMEDY (Singing and Dancing)
STYLE CLASSES FOR ADVANCED BALLET DANCERS

much of Butte County, has some of the richest agricultural land in the world and the

surrounding area also contains an abundance of recreational opportunities. Bidwell

Park, for example, is one of the largest municipally owned parks in the United States

(3,670 acres) and was the location for the classic 1938 film, "The Adventures of Robin

Hood" starring Errol Flynn. The city was founded in 1860 by General John Bidwell.

****

Chico is a nice little town, practically unknown except for the above-mentioned Errol

Flynn-*Adventures of Robin Hood* filming, the California State University campus itself,

and the fact that the campus was once voted Playboy's "Party School of the Year"! (The

administrators are still trying to live that one down.)

It's off the beaten path (even today you can't reach it by freeway) with a rather low-

key, out-in-the-sticks feeling. It was everything Harold was sure to hate in a city. He told

his friends it was "just above the Bay Area," but actually it's a hard, three-hour drive to

San Francisco. And Harold didn't drive.

Highway 99

The campus:

California State University - Chico began life as a small "Normal" (teaching) college, supplying schoolteachers to the rapidly growing Northern California towns of the late 19th century. Eventually it was renamed "Chico State College" and in 1970 became a state university when it was granted the right to confer graduate degrees.

Harold was not in the academic big leagues, but for someone with no scholastic achievements he had been lucky enough to find a job. Now, how much was he willing to put up with to keep it?

In the beginning there was great hope. An enthusiastic set of dance students made up a performing group that worshipped Mike and Harold and later became the nucleus of the new department. Harold was asked to direct a production of *On The Town* and help choreograph other musicals, dance shows, operettas... whatever was needed. They were trading on his name, and he was trying to wrap himself in an ivory-tower security blanket. It was an arrangement that looked rocky from the beginning.

In 1973 he suddenly got the offer of a show; a musical revue of George Gershwin songs to be called *The Gershwin Years*. Already signed up were Barbara Cook, Julie Wilson, and Harold's old pal Helen Gallagher. Was this the ticket back into the "big time?" It was only a summer tour and he wouldn't miss any required class time at the university, but what happened if it was a hit? What if it was slated for a Broadway -- or even an off-Broadway -- run? What would he do? The department heads worried they'd made an investment on him only to lose him whenever the chance of a professional comeback showed up.

The show warmed up with a couple of Western and Midwest dates, began in earnest in Philadelphia, and played the East coast summer circuit from May thru

September. Not successful enough for more performances, it did result in a few tentative offers the following year for other small-scale shows. One sounded good, but it would mean leaving Chico before the term was over for rehearsals and tour dates. No problem, he thought. Other instructors arranged to have their classes covered if they needed to be away for conferences and other activities that would also bring honor to the campus, surely he could have someone cover a few ballet classes for an opportunity like this?

No, he couldn't.

There were already undercurrents of disapproval for the rather cavalier manner that Harold showed toward his academic responsibilities and the way he treated his compatriots in the department. With a new-found feeling of security the old brashness returned. After all, he was the "star", weren't they lucky to have him? Later he would tell dark stories of departmental jealousy; how his last, best hope for a revival of his career cut short by the powers that refused him an early exit from the term. This has brought an unqualified denial from the department and I believe the truth is that the conflicts could never have been resolved gracefully, given the temperaments involved. Theatrical and academic circles are strangely similar in their egos, cliques, and back-stabbing plots. Professors can be even bigger divas than performers.

Harold's concession to the department of Speech/Drama/Dance (as it was called at the time) had been to sign up for classes himself and gradually work toward some kind of degree. His pledge to maintain even these simple requirements was a token one; although he dutifully signed up for a few classes he seldom attended and rarely received credits for any of his coursework. Usually he managed to charm and bluff his way through classes then get lots of help on whatever papers were due. Once he took an "incomplete" for a Music Appreciation" term paper and promptly forgot all about it until the "i" on his grade card eventually turned to an "F." Knowing how that was going to show up with the department faculty, he went begging for help to an old friend. I'm not sure what kind of grade he got out of the class, but what kind of music teacher could fail a student after getting a letter from Leonard Bernstein?

The department faculty began losing its collective patience with the resident ex-Broadway star, and in time a performer-vs-professor war was underway. Mike Madill had somehow managed to waltz his way to at least a Masters Degree and tried to keep a foot in both camps, but it was a battle Harold could never completely win. He hated schoolwork as much as he had as a kid, and stayed on the faculty's meager good graces by constantly maintaining full student rosters in a department that desperately needed the headcount to offset the less popular offerings, like, say, Classical Rhetoric. They also depended heavily on the dancers when mounting the Pioneer Week Musical, the year's largest theatre production.

CSU-Chico Performing Arts Center *(PAC)*

Harold and Mike were adored by the students, and we probably made the situation worse with our loyalty to the "Performers." The fact that dance majors later attained professional careers in greater proportion to the other theater graduates of the period shows that Mike and Harold must have been doing something right, but it wasn't enough to keep the department from finally transferring the dance program on Physical Education in 1974. It was a secret decision; Mike and Harold were told in a sudden faculty meeting and the students found out when it was a *fait accompli*. The classes remained, for the most part, in the converted storage closet under the first floor of the PAC (Performing

Arts Complex), but there was no longer a combined theater-dance degree. Harold pretended to be glad; he was no longer under the thumb of a department that he thought was being run by third-rate theater wannabes. The truth was he felt humiliated, and was too afraid of being back on the streets if he resigned. A few years later, when his mother died, he and his brother decided to sell the old house in Daly City. His half of the money would be saved, he told me; it was his "Fuck You" money. What did he mean by that? If there was ever another push-comes-to-shove conflict on campus, he could say, "FY" and take early retirement. He'd get that cottage in Carmel, write his autobiography and maybe have another chance to do the occasional tour.

Meanwhile, I was still a graduate student with a foot in both camps. Since I'd been accepted under the Speech/Drama/Dance umbrella, my program was safe but the strain of dealing with the unfairness of it all took a lot out of me. I did a Masters production, took a tentative degree and retired to teaching to cool off for a few years. When I did come back, it was with the idea of using Harold's stories of making *Fancy Free* into a Masters Thesis that even a faculty as biased as the present one couldn't turn down. Position: there was only one time in theatre history when a ballet was turned into a musical comedy which was in turn made into a music film. Had anyone every written about this fact before? Not that I could find. Also, luckily, not that any of the faculty could recall. Therefore there was no reason to deny my thesis topic: *Fancy Free and On The Town*, but I couldn't expect any real enthusiasm, either. They saw it as what it was, a slap in their collective faces for the shabby treatment the dance department received three years earlier.

Yes, Harold Lang was an instructor at CSUC, but he could not be named as part of my graduate committee because of his lack of academic credentials. Translation: if you only have a high-school diploma you are not qualified to judge post-graduate material.

Because of the special circumstances, however, they would consider him an "unnamed" member of the panel. Fair enough. The others would be Dr. Larry Wismer (my assigned graduate advisor; the most powerful person in the department and Harold's nemesis from Day One) and Dr. Gary Collier, a speech professor who was kindness itself and famous for having the most disreputable-looking office on campus.

I wrote my thesis, and just for good measure, dedicated it to Harold. It was accepted and a day was set for my oral examinations.

For those of you unfamiliar with oral examinations for graduate degrees, let me explain that you prepare for them pretty much as if you were facing Judgment Day a little ahead of schedule. In theory, anybody can attend and ask you any question that would be considered in the scope of your discipline. I remember the story of one theatre student who was defending a thesis being suddenly asked which who their favorite 18th century playwright. Already on the verge of a nervous breakdown from preparing for the day, the student drew a complete blank. After a long silence, the terrified candidate said quietly, "I don't think I liked anyone in the 18th century," walked out of the room, and was never seen again.

After hearing stories like this and seeing the preparations that had gone into other examinations (the conference rooms reserved, the professors making time to attend as if it were a sporting event) it's no wonder that I showed up on campus the day of my exams expecting the worst. I was sure they would make an example of me. I was sure they would take the added opportunity to have Harold in front of a bunch of *real* professors who know how to ask difficult questions about the Art and History of Theatre. I was prepared for everything but what I found.

Luckily, I was several hours early. Having to drive the forty miles from home and worried about not making it on time, I arrived at the Theater Arts department and found:

(a) no room reserved and (b) no notice of the examination listed. In short, no one outside of my committee and myself seemed to know what was happening, and I could only hope *they* remembered.

Walking rather desolately down the first floor hallway, I happened to see the "new guy," Dr. Randy Wonzong, sitting in an office they'd created for him from a lighting closet. I stepped in. Did he know about my orals that afternoon? He looked up, amazed. No, he hadn't heard anything about it. Seeming a little perturbed, he grabbed my copy of the thesis, promised to go through it during lunch, and... where was the exam being held? I told him I had no idea. Dr. Wismer wasn't in, but I supposed we'd meet at his office when the time came and see what arrangements he'd made. Then I turned around and drifted rather numbly back down the hallway, leaving him looking a little stunned.

At 2pm , a glum group consisting of Harold, Dr.s Collier and Wonzong and myself were lined up, waiting in the hall for the head of the graduate committee. Dr. Lawrence ("Larry") Wismer arrived, looking jaunty and quite pleased with himself (although a little taken aback to see Randy Wonzong) and announced that he'd planned to have the orals held in a "comfortable, informal setting;" that is, on the benches under the stairway in the back of the empty Adams Theatre. We all silently followed him the short distance from his office to the examination site and tried to make ourselves comfortable. In the meantime I saw Harold had turned to ice. He realized now why these orals were being kept so "informal."

Dr. Wismer began the proceedings by lightly dismissing my thesis as "finally having been completed" and that, since he was sure everyone was in agreement that there was no obstacle to my matriculation, I should be granted the Master of Arts degree as soon as possible. In effect, he was willing to give me my degree if only I would get out of his thinning hair ASAP. Gary Collier just looked down at the floor. He'd worked with Larry a long time and knew a brick wall when he ran into one.

Not so fast, Dr. Wonzong interjected. Someone needs to be actually *examining* this candidate before our department just hands her a Masters degree.

Oh well! Dr Wismer shrugged his shoulders, crossed his arms, leaned back against the wall and turned to Randy as if to say, "The floor is all yours."

Dr. Wonzong proceeded to ask me some questions about the research material in the thesis, forcing me to defend the points I'd made. (It was amazing how much he was able to come up with over lunch!) I gave him my answers; it was tough but it was what I'd been expecting, almost looking forward to. I don't think I can ever thank him enough. That piece of paper wouldn't have meant quite as much to me today if he hadn't made me feel like I had to fight for it.

When I was through, Harold cleared his throat and announced that he had something to say. With a look of astonishment and about as much good grace as he'd shown Randy, Dr. Wismer yielded the floor to him and sat back with an amused little smile.

Harold looked straight through Dr. Wismer and everyone else there. Very coldly he said only that he was pleased with my work and planned to make it required reading for his upper-level students.

What? Dr. Wismer said in mock amazement-- are you saying that this is a thesis that someone will actually *read*?!

For the first time that day Harold looked at him, the small-town professor who could never forgive Harold for having the career instead of the credentials. Yes, he said, that is exactly what I mean. And that was the end of my oral examination.

We all got up and walked out of the empty lobby. In the sunshine of the portico, everyone congratulated me on my Master of Arts degree. Harold shook my hand, turned and headed for LaSalles where there was a double shot waiting for him.

Later, Dr. Wonzong would take over control of the department, running it with diplomacy and skill for many years. I only wish he'd been able to show up a few years earlier. Maybe we could have remained a Speech/Drama/*Dance* Department.

****

Setting: Harold's small, one-bedroom ground-level apartment in Chico, California. I'd been a fan of Agnes de Mille's books, *Dance To The Piper*, *And Promenade Home*, etc. for years before I met Harold. Her descriptions of life on the road with touring ballet companies in the 1940s were more of an education into the world of dance than all the lovely photos in the coffee-table books I'd collected for years, but I was surprised at Harold's response to my enthusiasm. "Agnes is a naughty girl. Sometimes she doesn't 'remember' things right." That was about as harsh a statement as I'd ever heard him make about a famous colleague.

The thought that any of her work was fabricated -- or even that she would stoop to poetic license -- hit me hard. I thought about it for a minute. "It really doesn't matter, Harold. She wrote down, it's been published, now it's history. Unless you write your own version that's the only way it's going to be remembered."

"I am going to write my own book," he said, deadly serious. "That's what I'm going to do when I retire."

****

THE CENTRAL CITY OPERA HOUSE ASSOCIATION

proudly presents

BARBARA COOK   NANCY DUSSAULT
HELEN GALLAGHER   HAROLD LANG

in

THE GERSHWIN YEARS

music by GEORGE GERSHWIN

lyrics mostly by IRA GERSHWIN

with

STEVE ROSS   EDWARD MORRIS

direction and choreography by BOB HERGET

production supervised by DENNIS COONEY

from a concept by ARTHUR WHITELAW and PAT BIRCH

musical direction and vocal arrangements by EDWARD MORRIS

musical arrangements by MESSRS. MORRIS and ROSS

all musical compositions licensed by Chappell & Co., Inc. and Warner Bros. Music

special thanks to Edward Yablonski and Lawrence Stewart, special consultants,
Doubleday and Company, publishers of "The Gershwin Years"

Master Electrician: Thomas Seymour; Master Carpenter: William Downs; Master of Properties: Frank
Gates; Set Design: Boyd Dumrose; Assistant Designer: David Buzza; Constructed in Central City under
the supervision of Boyd Dumrose and David Buzza; Production Stage Manager: Mark Wright.

from DANCE Magazine, March 1975:
 the three sailors from the original cast of *Fancy Free*
take a bow at the American Ballet Theatre's 35th
birthday gala, "a marvelous moment."

Jerome Robbins, John Kriza and Harold Lang.

who's who for "the gershwin years"

BARBARA COOK
Barbara Cook made her Broadway debut as the ingenue lead in *Flahooley*, then played Ado Annie in the national company of *Oklahoma*, and appeared in *Carousel*. Her performance as Carrie Pipperridge brought her to the attention of the New York critics, and led to her first Broadway starring role in *Plain and Fancy*. She then played the role of Cunegonde in Leonard Bernstein's *Candide*. Miss Cook also starred in *The Music Man*, for which she won a Tony Award in 1957, *She Loves Me, The Gay Life, The King and I,* a second revival of *Carousel* in which she played the role of Julie, and the New York State Theatre production of *Show Boat*. Her most recent appearance was in *The Grass Harp*. In addition to the eight original albums she has recorded, she has also made two albums of compilations of Jerome Kern and George Gershwin songs, as well as *Songs of Perfect Propriety*, a collection of Dorothy Parker poems set to music, and a studio recording of *The King and I*. Aside from her work in the musical theatre, Miss Cook enjoyed a season of playing *Any Wednesday*, after which she appeared in the original Broadway production of Jules Feiffer's *Little Murders*. Miss Cook's most recent appearance was in Gorky's *Enemies* with the Repertory Theatre of Lincoln Center.

NANCY DUSSAULT
As a student, Nancy Dussault was a recipient of the *Young Artists Award* of the Society of American Musicians, and twice was guest soloist with the Chicago Symphony. Graduating in 1958, off-Broadway called; first for *The Boyfriend*, and then in *Diversions*. She joined the New York Opera Company, appearing in *Carmen, Street Scene, The Mikado,* and *The Cradle Will Rock*. Then, Nancy was signed to her Broadway debut in the musical *Do, Re, Mi*, playing the ingenue lead opposite Phil Silvers and Nancy Walker. Her performance won the Theatre World Award and she was nominated for a Tony Award. She then stepped into the Mary Martin role in *The Sound Of Music* for its final year on Broadway. In 1965, Nancy co-starred in *Bajour*. Once again she was signaled out for a Tony nomination. Nancy has since starred as Carrie in the New York City Center revival of *Carousel*, the lead role of Polly in *The Beggar's Opera* for N.E.T., and scored two successive triumphs, starring first in the New York revival of *South Pacific* and in Joseph Papp's highly acclaimed production *Trelawney Of The Wells*. The latter production was attended by Carl Reiner who quickly signed her as a regular on *The New Dick Van Dyke Show*.

HELEN GALLAGHER
Helen Gallagher won the coveted Tony Award (her second) as Best Actress in a Musical for her dazzling performance in *No, No, Nanette*.
Before appearing as the funny and pregnant Agnes Gooch in *Mame* for the St. Louis Municipal Opera opposite Jane Morgan and in the same smash musical at Kansas City Starlight Theatre opposite Gretchen Wyler, Miss Gallagher received tremendous critical acclaim for the same role on Broadway where she cavorted for two seasons opposite such *Mames* as Janis Paige, Miss Morgan and Ann Miller. Before that, the versatile singer-dancer-comedienne split her talents between her own role of Niki in *Sweet Charity* for which she received a Tony nomination and replacing Gwen Verdon in a starring role.
Miss Gallagher, true to theatrical tradition, rose from the ranks of the dancing chorus, first gaining recognition with a comic tango in *High Buttoned Shoes*. She went on to perform in *Touch and Go, Make a Wish, Pal Joey,* which not only won her a Tony Award for Best Supporting Actress in a musical, but the starring role on Broadway as Hazel Flagg. Next followed several seasons of night club and television appearances, returning to Broadway to star as Gladys in *The Pajama Game*.
If these do not make her familiarity seem logical, then picture her smiling face on a box of soap, can of wax or singing *Take Me Along* on television.

HAROLD LANG
Carrying a spear in a San Francisco Opera Production gave Harold Lang a taste of greasepaint and the urge for new expression. He became a dancer, went to New York with *Ballet Russe de Monte Carlo*, later toured with Ballet Theatre. In the Broadway musical scene he has appeared in *Mr. Strauss Goes to Boston, Three To Make Ready, Look, Ma, I'm Dancin',* then the original *Kiss Me Kate*. A fling at ballet again with the New York City Ballet's sensational London appearance, then back to the States to play *Make A Wish*, then the title role in the big revival of *Pal Joey* in New York, on tour and in London. After *Pal Joey* he did Saroyan's play *Time of Your Life* in New York, the musical *Shangri-La*, the musical *I Can Get It For You Wholesale*, then came two years in the Cole Porter revue, one year in New York and one in San Francisco. For the past three years, he has been teaching at California State University, Chico, in northern California.

BOB HERGET (Director)
A graduate of the Royal Academy of Dramatic Arts, Mr. Herget has directed and choreographed for Broadway, television, concerts, nightclubs, summer stock, and industrial shows. In New York his shows included: *Happy Hunting, Mr. Wonderful, A Family Affair, Something More* (with Barbara Cook), *Show Me Where The Good Times Are, All About Love,* and *The Boys From Syracuse*.
In the nightclub field Mr. Herget has produced acts for many stars as well as the premiere for Caesar's Palace in Las Vegas and the closing show for the Latin Quarter in New York.
In television Mr. Herget staged the *Yves Montand Special* which was nominated for an Emmy Award. Over three hundred shows later, he staged the *25th Anniversary Tony Awards Special*.
Summer theatre audiences will best remember his tour shows of the past two seasons, *Good News* with Alan Sues and *W.C.* with Mickey Rooney.

EDWARD MORRIS
Edward Morris has played and conducted four separate productions of *Jacques Brel Is Alive And Well And Living In Paris*, including the original in New York. He has recently embarked on a second career as comedy-writer and stand-up comic. As a writer he is represented on Lily Tomlin's Album, *And That's The Truth*.

STEVE ROSS
A seasoned performer, Steve Ross' recent one-man concert at The Washington Theatre Club in the nation's Capital drew rave reviews and high audience acclaim. His musical version of *King Kong*, called *The Ape Over Broadway* is scheduled for production next season.

HAL TINE (Set and Lighting Designer)
Mr. Tine is a graduate of the Carnegie Institute of Technology in drama. He has designed the sets and lighting for over fifty productions. His New York credits include *A Song For The First Of May* and *Please Don't Cry And Say No*. Mr. Tine has been associated with the Berkshire Theatre Festival in Stockbridge, Mass., where he designed the sets for *The Enemy Is Dead* in 1970 and *The Gershwin Years* earlier this season.

-7-

Every city has its diehard ballet students; the ones with enough love to donate a huge part of their lives to the art but without the talent or ambition to try for a professional career. Most of these people, along with the younger crowd who are "trying on" the life of a dancer to see if it suits them, become part of a community ballet company. Just mention the words *en pointe, arabesque, etc. etc.* and you'll know if you're dealing with someone who always secretly yearned to dance *Swan Lake* with the American Ballet Theatre. It was impossible for these people not to seek out someone with the background of a Harold Lang. He had been part of the Golden Age of the Ballet Russe and he had danced in nearly every ballet in the period's repertory. Having his name attached to a young, grass-roots organization was a monumental achievement.

The Chico Community Ballet would be his last ballet company. A current website outlines their 24-year history, but there is no mention of Harold Lang. Not in the history, not even in the bio given for one of the company's artistic directors, who was also one of Harold protégés and assistants. No mention of his encouragement, continual open house policy and free dance classes. Was any ex-student ever turned away from his home or his dance studio? I don't think so. *Mi casa, su casa.* How do you explain the sudden lack of interest on the part of people who were once proud to be his friends and so grateful for his assistance? Who say they don't even know where he is buried when they've lived within walking distance of his grave for twenty years? As childish as Harold could be in his endless search for amusement, I think anyone who knew him would give him credit for a better kind of loyalty and affection for his friends.

Giving Harold credit for his choreography, or expecting that any of his dances would still be performed today... that's a different story. Here was something that both the university's faculty and most of Harold's students realized quickly - that he was not a talented choreographer. When rehearsing for *Kiss Me, Kate*, the great Hanya Holm had asked the dancers to contribute to the show's choreography by improvising – in their own styles – to the music they would be dancing to in the show. This was her usual way of beginning a collaboration with the performers, and most of the dancers responded enthusiastically... except for Harold. His reaction at the time was along the lines of, "Just tell me what to do and I'll do it -- but don't ask *me* to figure it out for you!" It implied she wasn't doing her job. The other dancers passed it off as petulance on Harold's part, and probably no one but Hanya herself realized the truth; Harold was incapable of creating something original. His talent was in taking someone else's creation and tailoring it to his own style and body. Dance was a form of narcissism for him, and creation required an entirely different set of talents. When he was finally forced to put his name on a dance, it was composed of bits and pieces of ballets from his memory archive. That, and what the dancers themselves brought to the rehearsal. His name on the program as choreographer was what mattered. Often, at the university, when he was called on by another faculty member to contribute a piece of choreography for a production, he would pass it off on to a student who he knew would be thrilled with the opportunity.[1]

He was also a less-than-adequate dance instructor. Yes, we loved and appreciated his classes, but we all knew he could not teach ballet. For beginning technique you had better go elsewhere, or if you took Harold's beginning classes you had better get one of the advanced students taking the class as a warm-up to help you along. What you could learn from watching Harold was something else. Although he never "danced" his classes, there was an incredible feeling of "Aha!" in watching him give a combination. Something he would say, a position of his hand or even the turn of his head and you saw a series of steps as a performance. He *knew*.

---

[1]This is the way I was able to choreograph the "Tavern Scene" for the Music Dept's production of *Carmen*. I was in seventh heaven that Harold Lang had called on me to cover for him, but now I realize the director must have been furious.

But he also knew where he was and who he was dealing with. Sometimes I'd see him focusing on a spot over our heads on the back wall as we danced in front of him, never commenting on our inability to perform the same steps he remembered learning so many years ago. Every semester there would be more clumsy, beginning or half-trained students. Every year the ones who had reached any degree of proficiency would graduate and leave Chico behind. Some would actually go on to careers in dance, although none as successful as Harold's had been. From time to time these prodigal children would return, often when they were "between engagements" from the national touring companies of *Chorus Line* or *42nd St*. The door was always open and his couch made into a futon bed.

Besides these footnotes of his life, the years were going by without leaving much of a mark on Harold. When we showed up at his apartment only the faces of the excited undergraduates had changed; the host never did. After my Masters degree was completed, I began thinking of using him as a springboard to a doctoral degree.

Stealing one of my dad's new cassette tape recorders, I started interviewing him in the evenings when it was just the two of us. I had no experience in interviewing techniques and no particular skill in managing electronic devices, so it's a wonder anything remains of those hours. How could I have known I was sitting in on the last few years of Harold's life?

In March of 1975 something exciting had happened. The American Ballet Theatre held its 35th anniversary celebration, and Harold actually showed up. During a performance of *Fancy Free* the lights dimmed, and when they came up the three original sailors were onstage.

As Walter Terry tells it:

Fernando Bujones…, Buddy Balough and Terry Orr were the three sailors in an excerpt from Jerome Robbins's "Fancy Free", and as they finished, three gentlemen in evening

dress came on stage and executed a step or two -- they were the original sailors:
Robbins himself, John Kriza, and Harold Lang.[1]

The audience had gone wild as, for the last time, Harold took a bow with Robbins, Kriza, composer Leonard Bernstein and designer Oliver Smith (sitting in front). Back home we students would listen spellbound to Harold's stories of the evening.

And I never thought to get it on tape.

****

Then in 1978 we heard there was going to be a revival of *Pal Joey*. This was the era of all-black cast revivals of popular shows like *Hello, Dolly* with Pearl Bailey, and *Pal Joey* would star Lena Horne and Clifton Davis in an "updated," (God-help-us) *disco* version of the show that was doomed from day one. It did a West Coast warm-up to see if it was ready for Broadway, (it wasn't) and played in San Francisco's Civic Light Opera Series. Of course we all had to go. Lena Horne was an old friend of Harold's, and when he appeared at her dressing room door he told me she said, "Oh Harold! I'm so *sorry* about what we've done to your beautiful show!" I have the ticket stubs in front of me as I'm writing (August 26, 1978, Orpheum Theater) but I swear I have only a vague memory of the evening. It was such a disappointment I think I started blocking it from my mind on the way home.

****

Occasionally Harold would do a guest-teaching jaunt to Southern California during the summers off. In May of 1979 I received a letter from him about a book I'd told him

[1] I Was There, p/277

- 109 -

about that contained several mistakes:

Tues. May 8

Dear Danni,

I love teaching at Irvine and with a staff of 14 dance faculty I teach the most. 13 classes a week and the others teach from 3 to 10. The standards are high here, each teacher is different and they need my movement influence. I have a fine pas de deux class. They call "Modern Dance" - "Free Style" and also offer Baroque and Medieval dance. On weekends I teach at Tatiana Riabouchinska's studio in Beverly Hills. It is her company class - they are pure professionals, and a joy, even though it's an 1 1/2 hour freeway drive from here and we have the gasoline problem.

Gene will be annoyed at Agnes being given credit for "Billy." He's in New York and I'm staying in his house here. I'll tell him about the book. Michael Kidd didn't do "Fancy" until Jerry left the company to do a musical, a long time after the premiere!

I miss the charm of Chico. It's sterile but stimulating here but everyone commutes from other areas.

Can you read my printing? I miss my typewriter. Call me in July.

- Harold

****

September 13, 1979 was a day Harold had expected and dreaded for many years; his beloved mother, "Della," died at the age of 98. His mother had never given up on him and his happiest moments were in making her proud -- sharing his career with her as the return of her investment of devotion to him.

As much as he loved her, however, it had always been Al who had been there for her, nursing her when she was ill and making arrangements for her funeral. (Just as it would be Al who would do his best to share in Harold's last days and make the arrangements for his funeral. Years later Al would care for his terminally ill wife until her death, and then, with no one to care for and no one to care for him, he would almost immediately die himself.)

In 1979, at nearly 60 years of age, Harold was an orphan. He never really adjusted to losing his mother, the central-point of his life. Even then, five years before he was diagnosed with the cancer that would kill him, I think Harold lost the will to live. He was never quite the same and his drinking noticeably increased. Where before he could drink his students under the table, now he began showing the effects of the booze earlier in the evening. We got used to seeing him weave his way to the bathroom.

****

I was the one with the reference books that listed his birth date (real, that is -- he had several fake birthdates) as December 21, 1920. However, I don't remember whose brilliant idea it was to surprise Harold with a birthday cake on his 60th birthday.

Whoever was to blame, four of us (Tom Kinnee, Judy Zachai, John Rawlins and myself) showed up on his doorstep that evening holding a cake with candles lit, knocked on his door and yelled "Surprise" when he answered. How could we have been so stupid? Did we really think that a man who had lied about his age throughout the greater part of his performing career would appreciate being reminded that he had turned 60?

All credit has to be given to Harold; instead of slamming the door in our faces, he graciously invited us in, feigned delight (badly) and blew out the candles.

Our plan had been to sweep him up and take him out for dinner, but before we knew it the tables had been turned; Harold swept *us* (and a few other living-room regulars) up and took everyone out for a dinner that he didn't touch. I remember the glazed look in his eyes as he ordered the drinks and drank them on an empty stomach.

"Happy Birthday, Harold," I thought.

Harold, amazed by the light of candles from his 60th birthday cake,
Also, Judy Zachai and John Rawlins, friends and staff members from CSU-Chico.
(photo by author)

When you were alone with Harold, you were a special person. It didn't matter who you were, he made you feel *special*. You'd laugh yourself sick at his descriptions of your friends and classmates, and for a few hours he'd put you above them all. In his amusing, bitchy, backstage manner, everyone else was fair game for gossip. That know-it-all girl in the advanced class? A lesbian. My dear, didn't you *know* that? And your friend who's having the affair with her *much* younger partner. Why do you think she keeps giving him free... *lessons*?!! On and on, while he filled my wine glass and blew smoke in my face. And I hung on to every minute, knowing I'd be paying with a migraine the next morning.

If you were smart, you knew it was your turn to be the butt of gossip the minute you walked out the door. Nothing and no one was sacred, but if you really knew Harold you understood it was just his way. We were all the same to him – little nobodies basking in the attention of this guy who knew *everybody*. He referred to Leonard Bernstein as "Lenny!" In our small corner of the world Bernstein was someone you'd watched on TV since you were a kid; and Jerome Robbins, (he called him "Jerry"), was a dancer's god. How could we be anything but amazed to learn that Bob Fosse was Harold's <u>understudy</u> in *Pal Joey*? And how could we know how it must have cut Harold to the quick to see our amazement? After all, most of us didn't *really* understand that he had been a star once himself. We found books and old cast recordings in the college library and began looking at him through different eyes, but we were still too young to see how much our belated admiration must have hurt him. As far as we were concerned, he was history.

In 1982 I got a chance to invite Harold back to the dance room at Shasta College where we'd met twelve years earlier, this time with me as the instructor. He taught a master class that was exactly like all his Chico classes -- which meant I was the only one who knew what step was coming next. I was never a strong ballet dancer, but he went out of his way to make me look good in front of my students. That was also his way.

Lance   Thursday November 4, 1982

HAROLD LANG, head of the Chico State University Dance Department, performs in original production of "Fancy Free" with the American Ballet Theater. JEROME ROBBINS, choreographer, second from left, looks on.

Master dance class offered

Harold Lang, head of the Chico State University Dance Department, will hold a master class entitled "Dance for the Musical Theatre." It will be from 10 to 11:30 a.m. Saturday, Nov. 13, in the SC Dance Room. Cost is $10.

Students participating in the class may audition for his production number in the upcoming Winter Workshop at noon following the class. Lang has performed with the San Francisco Ballet, New York City Ballet, Russe Ballet, and the American Ballet Theatre. His Broadway productions include "Kiss Me Kate," "Pal Joey" and "I Can Get It for You Wholesale," with Barbra Streisand.

For more information, call Danni Bayles at the SC Dance Department, ext. 352.

NAME: HAROLD LANG   TERM: SPRING '85

	8:00	9:00	10:00	11:00	12:00	1:00	2:00	3:00	4:00	5:00	Eveni
Mon.					office	BEG. BALLET 1	BEG. Ballet 2				
Tue.			Styles	BEG. ballet 4	INT. BALLET 2		Office				
Wed.					Office	BEG. ballet	BEG. ballet 2				
Thurs		Styles 252 A	BEG. BALLET 4	INT. BALLET 3		office					
Fri.			office	INT. BALLET 4	ADV. BALLET 1						
Sat.											
Sun.											

Harold's last class schedule card (stolen from his CSU-Chico office door) June 1985

CHAPTER 8: 1984-85
LAST YEAR

Harold was sick. Really sick. When did we first start to take serious notice? It must have been at the time of his operation. Naturally, he played it down -- we only got vague explanations of why he as having surgery. He hated being seen as anything less than his own, vigorous, image of himself. Being hung-over had a certain romance; but being sick was just pitiful and Harold couldn't stand being pitied. Still, we'd had a feeling this was different, a definite turning point.

I sent flowers to the hospital and called after the surgery. His voice was weak, but straining to sound normal. I don't remember what excuse he gave for the whole procedure; somehow I knew it was bad. Before I hung up I said, "Harold, I love you." A stupid thing to say and totally out of character, since I knew Harold's mind didn't really grasp the concept of love. "I love you, too," he said. It was spoken like a line from a play, meaningful and meaningless at the same time. A few years before I'd gotten a Christmas card from him, inscribed, "Danni -- Hope you'll visit soon, mi casa es su casa. Harold" and then the next year's card said, "Where are you?" I hadn't had many reasons to drive the forty miles to Chico after finishing my Masters degree, and now I felt incredibly guilty. Sending flowers to the hospital was a bad idea, but I didn't know what else to do.

Once I'd made a remark that I wish he'd been my father and he was horrified -- not so much that I would see him as being a father-figure (which he was to so many of us) but that I could think of him as being *old* enough to have college-aged children! Getting old was not on his agenda, so he would "forget" dates whenever possible. Placing himself in a frame of history made calculations too easy, so he would lazily wave his hand, leaving trails of cigarette smoke in the air, and say, "Oh, I was never very good about dates." If you pressed him on an recorded place and time -- say, the opening of a show -- he would admit that was "probably right" but his demeanor would change and you'd feel the temperature of the room go down a degree.

He continued his usual schedule all semester, getting progressively thinner and weaker. He had a strange shuffle in his usual turned-out walk when he came down the halls of the PAC these days. By June it was obvious to everyone he wouldn't be teaching again in the fall, but no one wanted to confront him about it. Harold was dying; he knew it, we knew it, and he knew that we knew it. (Amazingly, his old colleagues from the faculty of the theatre department, who couldn't help passing him in the same halls, claim they had no idea he was seriously ill.)

I pulled out all stops and made the trip as often as possible to visit him. The legendary 100-degree-plus Sacramento Valley heat would be blazing and my car didn't have air-conditioning (unthinkable now!) so I would drive with one hand and spray myself from a water bottle with the other. Anxious for him to know how much it meant to me to be there I'd let him know all about the miserable drive, then kick myself because I knew his suffering was so much greater. Yet he never stopped being gracious to his guests, even though he'd never fail to turn around and poke fun at them to the next visitors. It was just Harold's way. Even so close to death he lived in the backstage bitchiness of the theater.

Only once when we were alone did he indicate to me what we both knew was happening. Out of the blue he began talking about when he first noticed something was wrong; describing how he had gone to the bathroom and noticed his stools were almost pure white. "Like clay," he said, then quickly added, "Oh, you don't want to hear this."

"Don't worry, Harold, my ex-husband was a registered nurse. When he was going through training I swear he'd save all the grossest parts of his day to discuss when we were eating dinner."

Harold looked visibly relieved. For a minute he'd let his guard down. That was bad enough, but it would have been so much worse if I'd shown disgust with his physical condition. The deterioration of his body was happening so quickly he was having trouble adjusting. His ankles and feet were swelling and the shuffling walk had become such a progressive dragging of one foot after the other; a complete embarrassment to someone whose life was centered on dance. When he had visitors he would only leave his seat to go to the bathroom. He couldn't stand being seen trying to walk without shuffling.

One well-meaning friend had brought him a stack of books on spiritual growth, life after death, and other metaphysical topics. "What do you think of all that?" Harold asked me, with a dismissive, smoke-laced gesture. This was late in the game; his body had shriveled and his face was taking on a scary death's-mask look. Checking the books gave me an excuse not to look at him. "I think a lot of it has merit, but some of it seems a little soppy, doesn't it?" I said, trying to think of what he wanted to hear. He took a deep drag from his cigarette and replied, "Oh, I don't know if I believe in any of it."

Did he believe any of it? I don't think I'll ever know, just as I don't believe anyone ever truly understood Harold Lang's heart. How could someone who didn't believe in anything face death as bravely as he did? Or was it because he didn't really face it at all -- he was simply playing another role? The last time I saw him (three days before his death), I hugged him. There was literally nothing there; nothing but clothing, a few bones and air... and Harold. Harold had never really gone away.

There are stories about the night he died, like that his last words were to poke fun at a woman who was one of his most devoted slaves. This is a classic "Harold" story and the one I want to believe; it shows that he remained the same bitchy person up the end:

He wanted to be in his own apartment, so a rotating group of friends were caring for him. He couldn't eat by this point... he couldn't even drink alcohol. All he could take in was soda pop laced with ground-up painkilling drugs. Even this he could only sip through a straw, and somehow the group caring for him on this particular night had run out of straws. A faithful lady-slave immediately took it on herself to race over to the neighboring grocery store, and I have no doubt she was graciously thanked by her master before she was out the door.

Minutes passed, and the friends in the room became preoccupied with conversation as Harold fidgeted. Finally he barked, "Where IS she?!"

When reminded that she had "run after his straws," Harold growled, "A hundred arthritic nuns could run faster than she can!" Everyone laughed. Not long afterward, Harold supposedly just put his head back, closed his eyes and died.

Thomas Steele's version was less flamboyant and probably much closer to the truth. Thomas was one of Harold's "new" friend's, having discovered the *mi casa* haven just as it became apparent its owners days were numbered. Being a rather mature and caring young man, Thomas volunteered his services as caretaker and was there to the end. His memory is that Harold began going downhill very quickly the last few days of his life. At one point, coming out of the bathroom, Harold remarked to Thomas, "Nothing works." Thomas asked if he should call the ambulance, and after a moment's consideration Harold answered, "Yes."

By the time the paramedics had made it to the apartment, however, he had reconsidered his options. Obviously his time was up, did he really want to end it in the hospital with all the breathing tubes and needles he detested? No, he was going to sit tight and die in his own little apartment. But in the meantime there were these nice guys from the fire department with their stretcher and medical equipment all ready on his floor; what to do? Being Harold, he entertained them.

First, he apologized profusely for sending them on a wild goose chase, offered them the hospitality of his home, and sent them away with jokes and laughter. When they were gone, he gave Thomas a check and asked him to run to the nearest liquor store for a bottle of champagne. Thomas kept the check ("It was Harold Lang's last autograph!") and paid for the wine with his own money. When he got back, they all sat around and talked about theatre and memories. Finally it was time for Harold to go to bed, while the others stayed and talked and waited. It was the evening of July 26, 1985.

If his death was hard for us, the funeral was a disaster. With all the best intentions in the world Al had found a minister and proceeded to give his brother a traditional Christian burial. It was everything Harold would have hated and we were all glad for once he really "wasn't able to make it." Al is gone now, too, God rest his soul; I hope the effort he put into Harold's funeral gave him comfort, because it left the rest of us feeling worse. The group I was with opted to skip the graveside service in favor of a private wake at the local ice-cream shop, something that we felt was more in the spirit of Harold's life. (Although a couple of beers would have been more appropriate.)

A committee was organized to create a Harold Lang Scholarship Fund for budding ballet students. My feeling was they were hoping to attract some of his "big name" friends into connecting themselves with the Chico dance scene. Whatever the motivation, the response was mostly low-key and local. A screening of *On The Town* was held at a benefit (how ironic, a movie showing for a man who could never get a film role), enough money was raised to send a few dancers to ballet summer camp, and the project quietly faded.

I never visited the grave until many years after I left the area. The cemetery isn't far from Harold's old apartment. I had a strong feeling of deja-vu as I went through Chico and the years rolled back. It was, of course, a miserably hot day. The summer heat in the Sacramento Valley towns often beats the Mojave Desert. I wandered the cemetery with a map from the office looking for the area they'd marked with a tiny "*x*" but thought I'd pass out from the heat before finding it. ("How appropriate, Harold. They could bury me right here, too.") Finally I flagged down a cemetery employee, but even with the two of us criss-crossing the area the location of the "*x*" remained a mystery. He offered to go back to the office for better instructions, but I suspected he was escaping to find some shade. Before he made it back I realized I was standing only a few feet from the grave. I pointed at the headstone in astonishment when he rejoined me.

"It was right here? How did we miss it?!" he asked. "We must've been walking over it for nearly twenty minutes!"

I couldn't help smiling. "Harold liked to play games," I told him.

CHAPTER 9: POST-MORTEM

After a college production, it's customary for the cast and crew to meet with the professors and hold what is affectionately called a "post-mortem." Like medical students we dissect the show, finding its weak points and being praised on what we were able to pull off in a hall-way professional manner. This is how we learn the craft of theater, by facing up to our mistakes (or blaming each other, which is also the way most professionals deal with criticism.) This is my post-mortem for my book, letting the reader know what I've done and what I wish I could have done better.

Too many things needed an author to be able to travel to research them completely. The Internet has been a wonderful information resource but the only was to access older records is usually by going to where the records are kept, and with my home and job it's been impossible to do that. I've tried to hire research assistants in areas across the country with little success. I'll always wish I could have done a better job finding more information on the 1945 Stamford summer performances and the various stock shows in the East and Midwest of the later 1950s and 1960s.

Also, there were disappointments in people who promised to come through with information, photos, etc. -- and then were never heard of again. That was hard. I didn't expect anyone to do it for me, but I hoped they would do it for Harold. My intention has always been that any profit from this book be put toward a performing-arts scholarship fund in his name. The materials I've collected over the years will be organized and donated to the UCLA Library Special Collections/Theatre Arts and titled the Harold Lang Archives.

****

APPENDICES

Harold Lang REMEMBERED

A Tribute To A Great Dancer And Teacher

Whether the student believed him or not, one thing is for sure: Bob Fosse never got on stage when Harold was scheduled to dance. In over 5,000 performances Harold Lang never missed a call.

Contrary to the stereotypical story of show business success, Daly City-born Harold Lang never wanted to be a star. In fact, he did not know what he wanted to do. Lang once told the story of how he was scolded one day by one of his teachers for having no direction. Feeling discouraged, he stopped at a cemetery on his way home from school to ponder the chiding. Whimsically, he gestured to the surrounding gravesites and said, "If any of you have something that you didn't get to finish, let me know. I don't seem to have anything to do." As he got up to leave he noticed a pair of crossed violins on the tombstone of the grave where he had been sitting. The young artist had died at age 30.

Within the next two weeks Lang, then working as a Western Union messenger boy, delivered a telegram to the building where the San Francisco Opera Ballet rehearsed. He asked if he could stay and watch. Seven months later he was performing there.

In dance, Lang once said, he experienced a "pure animal joy." As many people find, dancing soon can become an end in itself. "If I could have afforded it, I'd have been happy just to take class every day."

When Lang started to perform he discovered one of the great paradoxes of art. Pure technique, which is so satisfying to the dancer, bores the audience. Instead of just being a dancer executing steps onstage, Lang had to learn how to be a character

telling a story. "I discovered that there was a whole new discipline that I had to learn in addition to technique."

After a year as a lead dancer with the San Francisco Opera Ballet, under William Christensen, Lang joined the Ballet Russe de Monte Carlo. The Ballet Russe had one of the great traditions in classical dance going back through Leonide Massine to Fokine, Balanchine, Diaghilev and Petipa. The Ballet Russe was the first ballet company to capture widespread American interest and is credited with introducing classical dance to America.

In New York during the early 1940s Lang danced lead roles with Ballet Russe and the American Ballet Theater. At the time American Theater started to integrate the classical and popular traditions. In 1943 *Oklahoma* opened and with it a new page in American theater. The simple, bucolic story of Oklahoma settlers included Agnes de Mille's choreography. *Oklahoma* used ballet to reveal the dramatic undercurrents in the souls of ordinary people and forged a uniquely American art form.

Ballet Theater responded with *Fancy Free* in 1944. Just as *Oklahoma* brought high art into popular theater, *Fancy Free* brought theater into ballet. In place of otherworldly tales of mythical figures, Jerome Robbins created a story of three American sailors on leave. The ballet marked the first critical successes of Robbins and composer Leonard Bernstein, and Harold Lang, in the role of the First Sailor, joined in receiving 22 curtain calls on opening night.

Lang became one of the new breed of American entertainers who could move easily between classical art and Broadway theater. He created roles in *Mr. Strauss Goes to Boston*, *Look Ma, I'm Dancin'*, *I Can Get It For You Wholesale*, and Cole Porter's landmark success *Kiss Me, Kate*. He also made guest appearances with New York City Ballet and American Ballet Theater. In 1952 he scored his greatest success starring in the revival of the Rodgers and Hart musical *Pal Joey*. In 1947, 1948, and 1952 Lang received the prestigious Donaldson Award for the best dancer on Broadway.

I once asked Lang why he never went to Hollywood as so many of his contemporaries did. He answered that he could not give up the stimulation of a live audience. Although he had received several feelers from the movie industry, including one for the lead in the movie *Pal Joey*, which eventually went to Frank Sinatra, he never left the stage.

In the heyday of Broadway the collaboration of musicians, writers, and dancers created a stage art that broke down the barrier between the performers and the audience. Lennie Claret, one of Lang's dancer friends, said, "Broadway in those days was the greatest thing that ever happened in America." With the escalation of costs and correspondingly high ticket prices, that era now may be gone forever.

If there is a tragedy in this story, it is that Lang's 5,000 performances are now lost forever. There is

BY THOMAS STEELE

One Friday afternoon last spring several local dancers gathered at LaSalle's to talk shop over drinks and snacks. They had just taken Harold Lang's advanced ballet class at Chico State. As they scanned the menus and engaged in small talk, Lang grabbed a patch of moss from a potted palm tree, held it over his outstretched armpit, and said, "Look, a modern dancer."

Lang's lightning wit had struck again. Several of us almost fell off of our chairs with laughter. What we did not know at the time was that Lang was fatally ill with advanced pancreatic cancer. He died July 26 at age 64.

Dancers in the Chico area knew Harold Lang as a great wit and a generous friend and much more. Because dance has never developed a convenient notation system, it has evolved along the lines of an oral tradition. The nuances of style and technique must be given by the adept directly to the sweating apprentice. Thus the art has been passed down from teacher to student, choreographer to dancer, through the years. In Chico Harold Lang was a master to whom local dancers turned to find the roots of their art.

Lang's roots ran deep into the soil of dance history. Because of his natural modesty few people knew just how far his career extended. For example, one day a student was talking to one of her friends about world-renowned director and choreographer Bob Fosse. Harold overheard the conversation and, as he walked by, casually remarked, "Fosse, oh yeah, he used to be my understudy."

high ticket prices, that era now may be gone forever.

If there is a tragedy in this story, it is that Lang's 5,000 performances are now lost forever. There is rumored to be only one film of him dancing, and stashed somewhere in an archive. His special talent of turning in second position with his leg above waist level, his grand jump off the bar in *Fancy Free* and landing in a side split, from which he sprang as he touched the floor, and, if such things mean anything, his record of turning 15 pirouettes, are now the stuff of history books and dance legend.

I once asked Lang if he ever turned a triple tour. He said, "Sure, in class. But it happens so fast that the audience misses it. It's better to do a clean double and let them enjoy it." The audience always came first.

For the past 15 years Harold Lang taught ballet and musical theater at CSUC. To the hundreds of students he brought the great traditions of ballet and Broadway. To those who knew him well, he seemed less a hero than a wise father and great friend. He was especially proud of the dancers he helped into the professional ranks. His students could always depend on him for a helpful recommendation, a piece of sage advice, a couch to sleep on.

If there was one thing Lang hated, it was pretentiousness. In order not to compound the problem, he always attacked it with his keen sense of humor. During one conversation that had gotten a little highfalutin', he discreetly put a piece of paper into one of his nostrils and interrupted, saying "Excuse me, does anybody have a Kleenex?" That was Harold Lang. We will all miss him.

Thomas Steele was a student and friend of Harold Lang's. He lives in Chico.

Harold Lang (front with hat in hand) is shown here in a publicity photo leading the cast in the 1944 Broadway hit musical Fancy Free. (Photo/courtesy Thomas Steele)

August 25, 1985 CN&R

Harold Lang Remembered by Thomas Steele
Chico Enterprise-Record   August 25, 1985

Harold Lang Remembered

Several years ago Gore Vidal revealed that he associated Chico with two events in his life. The first was a hazy, brief stop in the middle of the night while his troop train took on water. The second was Harold Lang.

"Harold Lang?" I asked. "Yes," said Vidal, "the Harold Lang of *Look Ma, I'm Dancin'*" fame." Here I was a resident of Chico for over three years and ignorant of the fact that the person I saw in the 1952 Broadway revival of *Pal Joey* also had been a resident of our community since the early 1970s.

Vidal introduced us and, thereafter, whenever the chance arose, I made it a point to engage Harold in conversation. He was deeply modest by nature and small in stature, but to this former teenager the memory of him soaring through the air, hitting his mark, and yet all the while delivering his lines effortlessly, was beyond my comprehension. To make it as a dancer in a Broadway musical, I truly believed one had to defy the laws of gravity.

His obituary in the New York Times was commendable and praiseworthy. Understandably it focused almost exclusively on his stage career. But what of his post "footlight" years, especially those in Chico? Is there a legacy worth noting for posterity?

Although the opportunity for a "Harold Lang Recalls" program has passed, a "Harold Lang Remembered" type of program should be considered while our collective memory of him remains current. A local radio station executive told me that National Public Radio did a segment on him. But it, like the New York Times, originated in New York City and dwelled only on his early years. There is a lot of material right in this town for an enlightening program of local origin.

Had Harold Lang been a retired auto racer or rock star, I doubt if there would be any hesitation to document his work. But he was a teacher, and unlike Gore Vidal, he did not pass through Chico in the night, he stayed and enriched all of us.

John Gore
Chico

Harold Lang Remembered
by John Gore

Chico Enterprise-Record
August 25, 1985

Dear Sirs:

As the director of a dance company which employs only American dancers, designers, musicians and choreographers, I should like to bring to the attention of our dance audience certain alarming discrepancies in the vital problem of labor relations in the field of the ballet. A year ago, hearing the American Guild of Musical Artists was preparing to unionize this field, without compulsion and on my own initiative, I approached Mr. Ted Carr, the organizer, to make a contract for my American Ballet Caravan. This was done in time for our season with the American Lyric Theatre at the Martin Beck last May. Our contract specified that we pay twenty dollars week for rehearsal periods and a minimum of forty-five dollars a week on the road, with certain restrictions on traveling and rehearsal time. In October the Caravan commenced its second transcontinental tour from New York to Vancouver and back. The unionization of the company naturally made the tour considerably more expensive than on previous tours, but it is my opinion and experience that that, everything aside, it is more convenient to work on these terms. At the end of this tour, the following companies were also either on the road, or preparing to go on the road: The Monte Carlo Ballet, the Littlefield Ballet, the Joos Ballet, the San Francisco Ballet, the Kurt Graff Dancers, and Ted Shawn's Male Dancers. None of these groups had a union contract.

I was assured by Mr. Carr that every attempt would be made to Agmatize these groups. Due to internal conditions in the AGMA, which I hopefully believe have since been improved, the Monte Carlo came to New York and left without so much as a picket line or sympathetic protest from any of the affiliated Musicians, Wardrobe, Stagehands, or Company Managers Unions, ostensibly affiliated with AGMA.

It is not easy to finance weeks of work for American dancers on an American standard of living. The prestige of the international Russian companies is so great that $22.50 a week is considered average corps de ballet fair pay for a three-year contract, without restrictions as to rehearsal time or traveling conditions. Indeed, in some cases, American dancers are so fortunate as to themselves pay for the privilege of their presence in the Russian troupes. Now the Monte Carlo returns to New York for its spring season, without a union contract. What is the attitude of the American dancers and members of the dance audience to be? Actually, AGMA is in the unenviable position of supporting our native troupes, whether willfully or not. The foreign ballet companies, due to their staggering subsidy, accumulated reputation, and highly commercialized exploitation, have an overwhelming initial advantage over the native product. But due to their low labor costs, they can compete in the American market and defeat the less secure American groups, both by prestige and by pay.

The only other American company which is unionized under an AGMA contract is the Ballet Theatre, whose successful first season has been recently concluded at the Center Theatre. The Ballet Theatre and the American Ballet Caravan have upheld a standard which one hopes is not imaginary. But unless AGMA protects its own, the foreign companies can take advantage of the situation and further retard the American Dance.

Yours very sincerely,

Lincoln Kirstein

···

Editor's Note: It is indeed deplorable that no protection is offered our American companies who, in the true spirit of democracy place themselves under the jurisdiction of AGMA in order to insure the best working condition for their members. It is now apparent that they are automatically penalized by having set up standards which are so costly to maintain that they cannot compete with foreign groups which not only make no attempt to maintain standards but which obviously discriminate against American dancers and, in the end, take the money they make out of the country. It seems to us that considerable criticism attaches to AGMA in the situation an **The American Dancer** *for one, cannot accept the excuse that is being bandies about, i.e.: "until the Ballet Russe was out of town, no one thought to inquire if they were organized." We had an editorial on the subject written and, calling AGMA at the last minute to verify the fact that the Ballet Russe was unorganized (while they were still playing at the Metropolitan in New York) were informed by the young man who obtained full details as to our reasons for inquiring, that the CONTRACT WOULD BE SIGNED WITHIN TWENTY-FOUR HOURS. It being our deadline we accepted this assurance in good faith and thereby obligated them by failing to call public attention to the injustice being done our own dancers by the very group which should be their protectors.*

Look Ma, I'm Dancin'! (shown: original Broadway cast 78 rpm record set)

Music & Lyrics: Hugh Martin

Songs Featuring Harold Lang:
Decca (78) 24371 - *Gotta Dance* (with chorus)
Decca (78) 24373 - *I'm Not So Bright* (solo)

Notes: Recorded originally in 1948 as Decca Records no. 637. When reissued on 10" LP(DL 5231), an alternate version of the first song was used. This was also the version which appeared on the Columbia Special Products' re-issue thirty years later (X 14879), but the original 78 rpm version is available on Box Office Productions' "Three By Hugh Martin" (JJA 19743)

Kiss Me, Kate (shown: In 1948 *Kiss Me, Kate* was the first Broadway cast recording released in Columbia's new "LP" -long-playing - format, originally released as ML4140. Also reissued as S32609)

Music & Lyrics: Cole Porter

Songs Featuring Harold Lang:
Col (78) 55043 - *Why Can't You Behave* (with Lisa Kirk)
Col (78) 55043 - *Bianca* (solo)
Col (78) 55046 - *We Open In Venice* (with Alfred Drake, Patricia Morrison, Lisa Kirk)
Col (78) 55046 - *Tom, Dick or Harry* (with Lisa Kirk, Clay, Wood)

Notes: There was also a 78 RPM version [6 discs, 1949,Columbia C-200 (55042-55047)] and a 45 RPM version [5 discs, 1949 (Columbia A-200)], In 1958 an LP was released which gave credit for the television special, but is actually the original cast recording[Columbia OL 4140] and in 1963 a "fake stereo version was released [Columbia OS 2300]. The original cast members came together again in 1959 to record a stereo version in which Harold's tap-dancing can be heard on "Bianca. [STAO 1267]

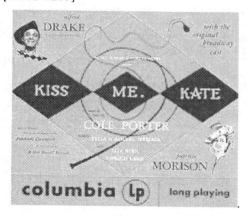

<u>Songs Featuring Harold Lang:</u>
You Mustn't Kick It Around
I Could Write A Book (with Fite)
Happy Hunting Horn
What Do I Care For A Dame?
In Our Little Den Of Iniquity (with Vivienne Segal)

Notes: Neither Harold or Segal were used on Capitol's "original cast recording" because of the earlier studio recording by Columbia.

Make A Wish *(shown: original cast recording,1951, RCA LOC1002. [Re-issued as RCA Red Seal CBM12033])*
Music and Lyrics: Hugh Martin

<u>Songs Featuring Harold Lang:</u>
Suits Me Fine (with Helen Gallagher)
Who Gives A Sou? (w/ Stephen Douglass, Nanette Fabray, Gallagher)
I'll Never Make A Frenchman Out Of You (w/ Gallagher)
That Face (w/ Gallagher)
Take Me Back To Texas With You (w/ Fabray, Gallagher)

The Band Wagon   *(shown: "Studio Cast" recording made in 1953)*

Music: Arthur Schwartz - Lyrics: Howard Dietz

Songs Featuring Harold Lang:
I Love Louisa (with chorus)
New Sun In The Sky (with chorus)

Notes: During the late 1950s. RCA recorded a series of 10" LP's called "Show Time, which featured songs from famous musicals. Broadway artists were hired to perform the numbers, but Bandwagon [RCA LPM-315] was the only one of the series using Harold Lang. The recording also shares disc space with "The Little Show."

Jerome Kern Revisited   *(shown: Studio recording made in 1956 by Columbia [OS2840])*

Music Jerome Kern (lyrics by various lyricists)

Songs Featuring Harold Lang:
Good Morning, Dearie! (with Barbara Cook, Cy Young)
Heaven In My Arms
Some Sort Of Somebody (with Nancy Andrews)

*Notes: reissued by Columbia in 1965 (OL644) and in 1990 by Painted Smiles (PS1363).
    Selection of songs by Kern, the legendary composer of such shows as "Babes In
    The Woods," "Showboat","Roberta" and films like "Swing Time" and "Cover Girl."*

I Can Get It For You Wholesale   (shown: original cast recording,1962 by Columbia [53020])

<u>Songs Featuring Harold Lang</u>
The Family Way (with Lillian Roth and cast)
Ballad of the Garment Trade (with Barbra Streisand and cast)
What's In It For Me? (solo)

Notes: Also available as Columbia KOS2180 and CBS Special Productions (AKOS2180)

<u>*The Decline and Fall of the Entire World as Seen Through the Eyes of Cole Porter Revisited*</u>

<u>Songs Featuring Harold Lang:</u>
I Introduced (with Kaye Ballard, Carmen Alverez and Elmarie Wendel)
I Happen To Like New York (solo)
What Shall I Do? (with Alverez and William Hickey)
Tomorrow (with Ballard and cast)
Farming (with Alverez and cast)

Notes: Original Off-Broadway cast recording made in 1965. Also included are several medley numbers with Lang and other members of the cast. Reissued by "Painted Smiles" in 1991 (PSCD124).

DISCOGRAPHY: MISC.

In addition to the subsequent releases of cast albums that I've included in the *Notes* sections, there have also been several compilation release that have include selections from "original cast recordings" (which sometime aren't). Most of the Harold Lang selections used on these later releases tend to be either from *Kiss Me, Kate* or *Pal Joey* and fall under the "Best of Broadway" kind of title. I am including just a few here but there are many more, and I'm sure the songs will recycled for many years to come.

- ***Broadway's Greatest Golden Hits*** (Disky B00005USEJ)

- ***Great Broadway Shows*** (Avid Records UK B0008FHP1E)

(The following represents only part of the research materials I've collected in preparing for this book. I am still in the process of cataloging the remainder before donating the entire collection to the UCLA Library Special Collections / Theater Arts)

Harold Lang Memorial Archives

BR: *Ballet Russe (de Monte Carlo)*
BT: *(American) Ballet Theatre*
CP: *"Decline & Fall Of The World/Cole Porter"*
CSU: *California State University (Chico)*
DC: *Daly City (early years, family)*
DTF: *Dayton Theatre Festival*
GY: *"Gershwin Years"*
ICG: *"I Can Get (It For You Wholesale)"*
KMK: *"Kiss Me, Kate"*
LM: *"Little Me"*
LMID: *"Look Ma, I'm Dancin!"*
MS: *"Mr. Strauss (Goes To Boston)"*
MW: *"Make (A) Wish"*
NS: *"No Strings"*
OUM: *"Once Upon (A) Mattress" - (National Touring Company)*
PJ: *Pal Joey ("PJ-L" London production)*
SFB: *San Francisco (Opera) Ballet*
SFWF: *SF Worlds Fair*
SH: *"Showboat"*
SL: *"Shangri-La"*
SN: *"Song of Norway"*
ss: *summer stock (Stamford, CT)*
TMR: *"Three (To) Make Ready"*
TYL: *"(The) Time (Of) Your Life"*
ZF: *"Ziegfeld Follies"*
misc. = misc. photos, materials (excerpts from books, etc.)
per = personal materials (including his death and funeral)

Year	Date	Type	Show	Description
1938	*n/a*	*brochure*	SFWF	Kodak brochure, 1938-39 Treasure Island World's Fair
1939	*n/a*	*misc.*	SFWF	"I Saw That" photo album, 1939-40 Treasure Island World's Fair
1939	*n/a*	*program*	SFB	1939 souvenir program, San Francisco Opera Ballet
1939	*3/2/39*	*flyer*	BR	BR at Shrine Auditorium; March 2, 1939
1939	*unknown*	*photo*	SFB	Harold, standing outside SF Opera House (taken by stage manager)
1939	*10/31/39*	*program*	SFB	copy of program notes & clipping: Oct. 31, 1939 (SF Opera House)
1939	*11/14/39*	*program*	SFB	copy of program notes: Nov. 14, 1939 (Pelican Theatre, SF)
1939	*11/18/39*	*program*	SFB	copy of program notes: Nov. 18, 1939 (Moore Theatre; Seattle, WA)

1939	*11/20/39*	*program*	<u>SFB</u>	copy of program notes: Nov. 20, 1939 (Royal Victoria Theatre, Canada)
1939	*11/29/39*	*program*	<u>SFB</u>	copy of program notes: Nov. 29, 1939 (Paramount Theatre, Salt Lake City)
1939	*unknown*	*program*	<u>SFB</u>	copy of program notes: (?) 1939 (Phoenix High School, Arizona)
1939	*unknown*	*program*	<u>SFB</u>	souvenir program; San Francisco Opera Ballet 1939-40 season (Harold in corps)
1939	*n/a*	*brochure*	<u>SFWF</u>	1939 Golden Gate Expo-World's Fair brochure, Wabash RR
1940	*2/6/40*	*program*	<u>SFB</u>	Oklahoma City SBOB performance (Harold in "Coppelia", "In Vienna")
1940	*n/a*	*brochure*	<u>SFWF</u>	1940 So. Pac. RR - San Fran. World's Fair brochure
1940	*n/a*	*brochure*	<u>misc.</u>	Golden Gate International Exposition travel brochure, May 25 - Sept. 29, 1940
1940	*unknown*	*photo*	<u>misc.</u>	early ballet studio shot for portfolio (seated on floor)
1940	*unknown*	*postcard*	<u>BR</u>	postcard of Ballet Russe performing at the Hollywood Bowl
1941	*unknown*	*photo*	<u>BR</u>	stage photo: "Saratoga", Harold leading company in Cakewalk section
1941	*unknown*	*program*	<u>BR</u>	Second Concert 12th Annual Season 1941-42 (no other date); Harold listed in "Nutcracker" (Trepak) and "Parisienne" (Soldier).
1941(?)	*9/20/41(?)*	*program*	<u>BR</u>	program: Royal Alexandra Theatre - Toronto, Canada (1941 - year is right if 9/20 is on a Saturday)
1941	*10/15/41*	*program*	<u>BR</u>	Ballet Russe at NYC Metropolitan Opera House; Harold in "Scheherazade" - , (adolescent)"Snow Maiden" (peasant) and "Le Beau Danube" (dandy)
1941	*10/19/41*	*program*	<u>BR</u>	Ballet Russe at NYC Metropolitan Opera House; Harold in "Rouge Et Noir" - Blue, "Saratoga" (jockey) and "Gaite Parisienne" (soldier)
1941	*n/a*	*program*	<u>BR</u>	1941-42 BR souvenir program (no photos w/Harold)
1942	*n/a*	*ad*	<u>BR</u>	ad for 1942-43 Ballet Russe tour (photo w/Harold in "Labyrinth")
1942	*n/a*	*program*	<u>BR</u>	BR souvenir program (photo w/Harold in "Labyrinth")
1943	*n/a*	*program*	<u>BT</u>	1943-44 BT souvenir program (photo of Harold in corps)
1943	*11/1/43*	*program*	<u>BR</u>	Ballet Russe at SF Opera House (Harold not listed)
1943	*12/8/43*	*program*	<u>BT</u>	Indianapolis (English Theatre); Harold listed in "Princess Aurora" (Attendant to Fairy and Pas de Trois), "Capriccio Espagnol" (Alborada)
1943	*12/14/43*	*program*	<u>BT</u>	Des Moines, Iowa - BT house program (Harold in "Mademoiselle Angot")
1944	*1/44*	*Stagebill*	<u>BT</u>	Chicago tour - Ballet Theatre
1944	*1/44*	*program*	<u>BT</u>	Chicago tour - Ballet Theatre
1944	*unknown*	*photo*	<u>BT</u>	copy photos of "Fancy Free" publicity shots
1945	*8/13/45*	*program*	<u>MS</u>	Boston tryout program: "Mr. Strauss Comes To Boston" (Shubert Theatre) - 2
1945	*n/a*	*program*	<u>MS</u>	Souvenir program, "Mr. Strauss"

1945	*n/a*	*book*	<u>MS</u>	1945-46 Theatre World ("Mr. Strauss" - pg. 10, "TMR" - pg. 78)
1945	*n/a*	*sheet music*	<u>MS</u>	sheet music for "Mr. Strauss Goes To Boston" ("Into The Night")
1945	*12/1/45*	*program*	<u>BT</u>	Chicago BT tour program; Harold not listed- why? (This was after "MS" and before "TMR")
1946	*unknown*	*program*	<u>TMR</u>	souvenir program, "Three To Make Ready" (first format printed)
1946	*unknown*	*program*	<u>TMR</u>	souvenir program, "Three To Make Ready" (second format printed)
1946	*unknown*	*postcard*	<u>TMR</u>	souvenir advertisement postcard, "Three To Make Ready"(Harold w/Jane Deering)
1946	*4/22/46*	*Playbill*	<u>TMR</u>	Playbill, "Three To Make Ready" (week of April 22, 1946)
1946	*5/20/46*	*Playbill*	<u>TMR</u>	Playbill, "Three To Make Ready" (week of May 20, 1946)
1946	*10/14/46*	*Playbill*	<u>TMR</u>	Playbill, "Three To Make Ready" (week of Oct. 14, 1946)
1946	*12/30/48*	*Playbill*	<u>misc.</u>	12/30/46 "Years Ago" Playbill article & ad for Waldorf-Astoria Wedgewood Room ("Deering & Lang")
1947	*1/13/47*	*Playbill*	<u>misc.</u>	1/13/47 "Red Mill" Playbill ad for Waldorf-Astoria Wedgewood Room ("Deering & Lang")
1947	*2/16/47*	*Stagebill*	<u>TMR</u>	Chicago Stagebill, "Three To Make Ready" (week of Feb. 16, 1947)
1948	*n/a*	*book*	<u>LMID</u>	1947-48 Theatre World ("Look Ma, I'm Dancing" - page)
1948	*2/28/48*	*Playbill*	<u>LMID</u>	Playbill, "Look Ma, I'm Dancin!" (week of Jan. 28, 1948)
1948	*3/1/48*	*Playbill*	<u>LMID</u>	Playbill, "Look Ma, I'm Dancin!" (March 1948)
1948	*6/14/48*	*Playbill*	<u>LMID</u>	Playbill, "Look Ma, I'm Dancin!" (week of June 14, 1948)
1949	*2/21/49*	*Playbill*	<u>KMK</u>	Playbill, "Kiss Me, Kate" (week of Feb. 21, 1949)
1949	*3/7/49*	*Playbill*	<u>KMK</u>	Playbill, "Kiss Me, Kate" (week of March 7, 1949)
1949	*3/1/49*	*magazine*	<u>KMK</u>	Theatre World Magazine (London), March 1949 issue; review and photos of Broadway's "KMK"
1949	*4/1/49*	*Theatre Arts*	<u>KMK</u>	Theatre Arts, April 1949 ("Kiss Me, Kate" - cover story)
1949	*?*	*program*	<u>KMK</u>	original cast souvenir program: "Kiss Me, Kate"
1949	*5/23/49*	*program*	<u>KMK</u>	house program, "KMK"
1949	*?*	*photo*	<u>misc.</u>	Harold with Bette Davis and Glen Ford (1949?)
1949	*n/a*	*program*	<u>BT</u>	1949-50 Ballet Theatre; 10th Anniversary program (Harold not in company)
1950	*2/27/50*	*Playbill*	<u>KMK</u>	Playbill, "Kiss Me, Kate" (week of Feb. 27, 1950)
1950	*5/15/50*	*Playbill*	<u>KMK</u>	Playbill, "Kiss Me, Kate" (week of May 15, 1950)
1950	*7/12/50*	*program*	<u>NYCB</u>	NYCB Covent Garden program/Harold in "Symphony In C" (3rd Movement, lead w/Janet Reed)

1950	*7/13/50*	*program*	<u>NYCB</u>	NYCB Covent Garden program/Harold in "Jinx" ("Equestrian")
1950	*7/21/50*	*program*	<u>NYCB</u>	NYCB Covent Garden program/Harold in "Symphony In C" (3rd Movement, lead w/Janet Reed)
1950	*7/25/50*	*program*	<u>NYCB</u>	NYCB Covent Garden program/Harold in "Jinx" ("Equestrian") & "Jones Beach" (4th movement, "Hot Dogs" w/ Melissa Hayden)
1950	*8/2/50*	*program*	<u>NYCB</u>	NYCB Covent Garden program/Harold in "Bouree Fantasque" (lead w/Tanaquil LeClercq)
1950	*8/5/50*	*program*	<u>NYCB</u>	NYCB Covent Garden program/Harold not listed
1950	*8/1/50*	*magazine*	<u>KMK</u>	London Theatre World review, NYC Ballet season (pg. 9 - no mention of HL)
1950	*8/21/50*	*CD*	<u>PJ</u>	recorded "Pal Joey" songs w/Vivienne Segal at NYC CBS Studios (info on CD from original 45s, although other information says September.)
1950	*9/5/50*	*program*	<u>NYCB</u>	NYCB Covent Garden program/Harold not listed
1951	*4/23/51*	*Playbill*	<u>MW</u>	Playbill, "Make A Wish" (week of April 23, 1951)
1951	*5/6/51*	*program*	<u>ANTA</u>	Anta Album, performed at Ziegfeld Theatre featuring Harold Lang, Helen Gallagher in number from "MW"
1951	*6/11/51*	*Playbill*	<u>MW</u>	Playbill, "Make A Wish" (week of June 11, 1951)
1951	*unknown*	*photo*	<u>MW</u>	stage photo: Harold w/3 cast members, sitting at table, "Make A Wish"
1951	*unknown*	*photo*	<u>MW</u>	stage photo: Harold and Helen Gallagher; curtain call w/Nanette Fabrey, "Make A Wish"
1951	*n/a*	*letterhead*	<u>MW</u>	show letterhead - 20 sheets (10 sent to Nanette Fabrey, April 2001)
1951	*n/a*	*sheet music*	<u>MW</u>	sheet music, chorus contract & photo of N. Fabrey
1951	*unknown*	*recording*	<u>MW</u>	original cast LP, "Make A Wish"
1952	*1/12/52*	*magazine*	<u>PJ</u>	LIFE magazine w/article & photos on "Pal Joey"
1952	*2/1/52*	*magazine*	<u>PJ</u>	DANCE magazine w/full-page ad & photo of "Pal Joey" (pg. 5)
1952	*unknown*	*program*	<u>PJ</u>	original cast souvenir program, "Pal Joey"
1952	*3/24/52*	*Playbill*	<u>PJ</u>	Playbill, "Pal Joey" (original cast: week of March 24, 1952)
1952	*3/31/52*	*Playbill*	<u>PJ</u>	Playbill, "Pal Joey" (original cast: week of March 31, 1952)
1952	*4/28/52*	*Playbill*	<u>PJ</u>	Playbill w/ticket stubs, "Pal Joey" (original cast, week of April 28, 1952)
1952	*6/1/52*	*magazine*	<u>PJ</u>	DANCE Magazine, June 1952 issue (cover photo: Harold in "Pal Joey")
1952	*6/1/52*	*magazine*	<u>PJ</u>	Theatre World Magazine (London), June 1952 issue; review and photos of Broadway's "Pal Joey"
1952	*7/7/52*	*Playbill*	<u>PJ</u>	Playbill, "Pal Joey" (original cast- week of July 7, 1952)
1952	*8/8/52*	*Playbill*	<u>PJ</u>	Playbill, "Pal Joey" (w/Holly Harris - week of Aug. 8, 1952)
1952	*8/16/52*	*Stagebill*	<u>PJ</u>	Chicago Stagebill, "Pal Joey" (Sam S. Shubert Theatre)

1952	8/20/52	Playbill	PJ	Playbill, "Pal Joey" (w/Holly Harris) standing room tickets attached (1.80/ea)
1952	n/a	record	PJ	set of 45rpm records, "Pal Joey"
1952	12/29/52	Playbill	PJ	Playbill, "Pal Joey" (original cast - week of Dec. 29, 1952)
1952	12/52	misc.	FF	"News From Home" (Home Insurance magazine) Holiday issue w/ballet theme; photo of Harold in "Fancy Free" pose, pg. 3
1953	1/1/53	calendar	PJ	Capezio calendar w/HL ("PJ") on July
1953	unknownn	Playbill	PJ	cover of "Pal Joey" signed by Harold & Carol Bruce (touring cast)
1953	unknown	program	PJ	Seattle Met Opera House program, "Pal Joey" (touring cast)
1953	n/a	program	PJ	souvenir program, "Pal Joey" (co-starring Carol Bruce)
1953	unknown	program	PJ	Playgoer cover only (Geary Theater) signed by Harold and Carol Bruce
1953	unknown	article	misc.	clippings from San Francisco papers, signed by Harold (re: "Pal Joey")
1953	unknown	photo	misc.	signed photo of Harold with Violet, wife of SF Opera House manager
1953	4/20/53	program	PJ	Washington, DC - Shubert Theatre, "Pal Joey" house program
1953	8/31/53	program	PJ	program/Greek Theatre/LA - "Pal Joey" touring company (Aug. 31, 1953)
1954	n/a	book	PJ-L	"Musical Comedy; A Story in Pictures" -- #207, "Pal Joey" London production
1954	n/a	misc.	PJ-L	London "Theatre World" - May 1954 ("Pal Joey" - pg.6-7)
1954	5/1/54	Plays&Players	PJ-L	full-page photo of Carol Bruce, pg. 5; review, pg. 10.
1954	5/1/54	misc.	PJ-L	"Gramophone" advertisement for Columbia Pal Joey cast album "featuring Harold Lang"
1954	n/a	record	PJ-L	Columbia #33SX-1027 Pal Joey cast album "featuring Harold Lang" - also: V. Segal, Barbara Ashley, Beverly Fife, Kenneth Remo, Jo Hurt
1954	n/a	program	PJ-L	Souvenir program, Dick France as PJ in London production
1954	9/54	TheatreWorld	PJ-L	Original London production of "Pal Joey" - 2
1955	1/24/55	Playbill	TYL	autographed program - "Time Of Your Life"
1955	4/55	Theatre Arts	TYL	April 1955 Theatre Arts, pg.s 22 & 25
1955	unknown	program	KMK-r	Souvenir Program for KISS ME KATE at the San Francisco Civic Light Opera, 1955 by Cole Porter with Jean Fenn, Robert Wright, Harold Lang, Pat Crowley.
1956	2/56	magazine	misc.	"Trim" vol. 1 no. 1
1956	4/21/56	Playbill	SL	copy of Playbill, "Shangri-La" w/autographs (week of April 21,1956)
1956	4/21/56	Playgoer	SL	copy of Playbill, "Shangri-La" - premiere, New Haven (week of April 21,1956)
1956	6/25/56	Playbill	SL	Playbill, "Shangri-La" (week of June 25, 1956)

1956	*8/56*	*TheatreArts*	<u>SL</u>	review, "Shangri-La," pg. 16
1956	*10/56*	*magazine*	<u>*misc.*</u>	Oct.1956 vol.2 no.4 - "Body Beautiful"
1957	*2/4/57*	*program*	<u>ZF</u>	New Haven opening program Shubert Theatre, "Ziegfeld Follies" (week of Feb, 4, 1957)
1957	*10/1/57*	*magazine*	<u>*misc.*</u>	Oct.1957 vol.3 no. 4 - "Body Beautiful"
1957	*2/4/57*	*Playgoer*	<u>ZF</u>	WORLD PREMIERE, February 4-9, 1957 "Playgoer" playbill - New Haven
1957	*4/22/57*	*Playgoer*	<u>ZF</u>	Playbill, "Ziegfeld Follies" (week of April 22, 1957)
1957	*5/27/57*	*Playgoer*	<u>ZF</u>	Playbill, "Ziegfeld Follies" (week of May 27, 1957)
1957	*6/10/57*	*Playgoer*	<u>ZF</u>	Playbill, "Ziegfeld Follies" (week of June 10, 1957)
1957	*n/a*	*book*	<u>ZF</u>	"Theatre World: Season 1956-57"
1957	*n/a*	*misc.*	<u>ZF</u>	sheet music for "Mangos"/Ziegfeld Follies
1957	*4/13/57*	*brochure*	<u>ZF</u>	Ticket Service, Inc. amusement listings for April 13, 1957
1959	*7/28/59*	*program*	<u>DTF</u>	house program, Dayton Theatre Festival; "Oklahoma!"
1959	*8/18/59*	*program*	<u>DTF</u>	house program, Dayton Theatre Festival; "Pal Joey"
1960	*8/1/60*	*program*	<u>OUM</u>	SF program for "Flower Drum Song" lists OUM coming w/Harold Lang
1960	*?*	*program*	<u>MF/NY</u>	house program, Melody Fair (N. Tonawanda, NY) ; "Pal Joey"
1960	*12/6/60*	*Playbill*	<u>OUM</u>	Playbill: St. Louis, "Once Upon A Mattress"
1961	*2/27/61*	*Playbill*	<u>OUM</u>	Playbill: Boston, Feb-March, "Once Upon A Mattress"
1961	*unknown*	*program*	<u>OUM</u>	souvenir program: National Phoenix Theatre Co., "Once Upon A Mattress"
1962	*2/12/62*	*Playbill*	<u>ICG</u>	Playbill: February 12, 1962 - Boston
1962	*unknown*	*Bravo*	<u>ICG</u>	Bravo, vII.n3, w/photo of Harold with Elliot Gould and Lillian Roth in "Sounds of Music on Broadway" section
1962	*5/16/62*	*LIFE*	<u>ICG</u>	Life magazine entertainment feature on "Wholesale"
1962	*5/28/62*	*Playbill*	<u>ICG</u>	Playbill: May 28, 1962 - Sam S. Shubert Theatre, New York
1962	*6/62*	*book*	<u>ICG</u>	London's "Theatre World" review of "I Can Get It For You Wholesale"
1962	*6/4/62*	*Playbill*	<u>ICG</u>	Playbill: June 4, 1962 - Sam S. Shubert Theatre, New York
1962	*unknown*	*photo*	<u>ICG</u>	photo (stage or rehearsal?) Harold & Barbra Streisand
1962	*n/a*	*book*	<u>ICG</u>	1961-62 Theatre World ("ICG" - pg. 86)
1962	*6/62*	*magazine*	<u>ICG</u>	London's "Theatre World"; review of "ICG" - pg. 24

1962	*9/3/62*	*Playbill*	<u>ICG</u>	Playbill: Sept. 3, 1962 - Sam S. Shubert Theatre, New York
1963	*unknown*	*program*	<u>SH</u>	"Showboat" - Milwaukee's Swan Theatre (?)
1963	*7/16/63*	*program*	<u>SN</u>	house program/"Song of Norway"; Warren, Ohio
1963	*7/16/63*	*program*	<u>SN</u>	souvenir program/"Song of Norway"; Warren, Ohio
1964	*unknown*	*program*	<u>NS</u>	souvenir program, "No Strings" (specific date, location unknown)
1964	*unknown*	*program*	<u>LM</u>	souvenir program, "Little Me" (specific date, location unknown)
1965	*unknown*	*book*	*<u>misc.</u>*	photos in "First Lady" (Patrick Dennis)
1965	*unknown*	*CD*	<u>CP</u>	"The Decline & Fall Of The World As Seen Through The Eyes Of Cole Porter"
1965	*n/a*	*poster*	<u>CP</u>	"The Decline & Fall Of The World As Seen Through The Eyes Of Cole Porter"
1967	*n/a*	*book*	*<u>misc.</u>*	Dance World 1967, v.2 w/ short bio on HL, pg. 200
1972	*1/72*	*program*	*misc.*	CSU-Chico *Look & Listen* show; Harold choreographed "California Scene"
1973	*unknown*	*program*	<u>GY</u>	copy of "The Gershwin Years" program from Central City, CO
1973	*unknown*	*tape*	<u>GY</u>	copy audiotape, "The Gershwin Years" (taped from audience)
1980	*12/22/80*	*photos*	*<u>misc.</u>*	photos of Harold's 60th birthday party (Dec 21, 1980 - Chico, California)
1980	*12/22/80*	*photo*	*<u>misc.</u>*	photo of Harold; Chico Ballet Xmas party (Dec 22, 1980)
1982	*12/82*	*program*	*misc*	CSU-Chico *Curtains Up* show; Harold staged "Pas de Trois" from *Swan:Lake*
1983	*unknown*	*article*	*misc*	Impulse magazine (CSU-Chico) article by Kris Bamman, "Chico's Broadway Connection"
1984	*2/84*	*article*	*misc*	"For the Record: Harold Lang" by Peter Lynch from SHOWMUSIC, v4,n1 (issn 8755-9560)
1985	*8/85*	*articles*	*<u>per</u>*	obituaries
1986	*5/6/86*	*program*	*<u>misc</u>*	Benefit film showing, "On The Town", Wall Street Dance Academy
2000	*7/27/00*	*letter*	*<u>misc.</u>*	Correspondence/Nanette Fabray
2000	*9/18/00*	*letter*	*<u>misc.</u>*	Correspondence/Arthur Laurants
2000	*10/21/00*	*letter*	*<u>misc.</u>*	Correspondence/Nanette Fabray
2000	*10/1/00*	*photo*	*<u>per</u>*	color photo of Harold Lang's grave (Chico, California)
2000	*12/30/00*	*letter*	*<u>misc</u>*	Correspondence/Carol Bruce
2001	*2/12/01*	*letter*	*<u>misc</u>*	Correspondance/FBI/Harold was not a "person of interest" in the '50s
2001	*3/18/01*	*letter*	*<u>misc</u>*	Correspondence/Carol Bruce

2001	*3/24/01*	*tape*	*misc*	Interview/Carol Bruce
2001	*7/26/01*	*email*	*misc*	Correspondence/Fred Kaplan, author of Gore Vidal biography
2001	*5/15/01*	*photo*	*misc*	Autographed 8x10 glossy, sent by Carol Bruce
2002	*9/12/00*	*letter*	*misc.*	Correspondence/Kaye Ballard
2002	*10/24/00*	*letter*	*misc.*	Correspondence/Fred Blumenthal re: Dayton summer theater, 1959
2003	*8/11/03*	*letter*	*misc*	Correspondence/Nanette Fabray
2003	*1/11/03*	*letter*	*misc*	Correspondence/Anon(re:1983 Houston gathering for Ballet Russes dancers

BIBLIOGRAPHY

Every effort has been made to acknowledge reference material used in this book, but in some cases authors could not be located or did not respond to my inquiries. If a question arises over the use of any material, I sincerely regret the error and will be happy to make corrections in a future edition.

BOOKS:

Ballard, Kaye. How I Lost 10 Pounds in 53 Years. Argent Books Boulder, Colorado. 2005.

Blum, Daniel. A Pictorial History of the American Theatre, 1900-1950. New York, Greenberg. 1950.

Chujoy, Anatole. The New York City Ballet. New York. Knopf, 1953.

Clum, John M. Something for the Boys: Musical Theater and Gay Culture. St. Martin's Press, 1999.

Constantine. Souvenir de Ballet. San Diego, Hester & Smith, Inc. 1947.

de Mille, Agnes. And Promenade Home. Boston: Little, Brown & Co., 1958.

deMille, Agnes. Dance To The Piper. Boston. Little, Brown & Co., 1951.

Denby, Edwin. Dance Writings. New York. Knopf, 1986.

Eells, George. Cole Porter: the Life That Late He Led. New York. G.P., Putnum's Sons. 1967.

Ewen, David. Complete Book of the American Musical Theatre. New York. Holt Rinehart & Winston. 1965.

Flinn, Denny Martin. Muscial! A Grand Tour. New York, Schirmer Books, 1997.

Gill, Brendon. Cole. New York. Holt, Rinehart & Winston, 1971.

Gottfried, Martin. All His Jazz: The Life and Death of Bob Fosse. New York. Bantam Books, 1990.

Gottfried, Martin. Broadway Musicals. 1979.

Grant, Martin N. The Rise and Fall of the Broadway Musical. Northeastern University Press, 2004.

Green, Stanley. Encyclopedia of the Musical Theatre. New York, Vail-Ballou Press, 1976

Hering, Doris. Twenty-Five Years of American Dance. New York, Rudolf Orthwine Publisher, 1954.

Hurtes, Hettie Lynne. The Backstage Guide to Casting Directors. New York, BackStage Books, 1992.

Kaplan, Fred. Gore Vidal. Anchor Books, 2000.

Laurents, Arthur. Original Story. New York, Knopf, 2000.

Little, Stuart Off-Broadway: The Prophetic Theater. New York; Coward, McCann &Geoghegan, 1972

Smith, H. Allen. Life In A Putty Knife Factory. Philadelphia; the Blakiston Co. 1943.

Steinberg, Cobbett. San Francisco Ballet: the First Fifty Years. San Francisco Ballet Assoc, 1983.

Stott, William and Jane Stott. On Broadway. Photos by Fred Fehl. University of Texas Press, 1978.

Teffault, Elizabeth M. Gayway. New York, Vantage Press, 1976.

Terry, Walter. I Was There: Selected Dance Reviews, 1936-1976. New York. Audience Arts, 1978.

Winn, Bernard. 'The Top Of The Hill': Growing Up in Daly City San Francisco. Incline Press, 1999.

PERIODICALS:

(anon) "Starring: Harold Lang." <u>Body Beautiful</u>: Oct. 1956, v2 n4

(anon) "Harold Lang: A TRIM Star." <u>TRIM</u>: Feb. 1956, v1 n1

Bammam, Kris. "Harold Lang, Chico's Broadway Connection." <u>CSUC Impulse</u>: Spring 1983.

Gottlieb, Beatrice. "Balanchine's Ballet." <u>Theatre Arts</u>: Oct. 1951, v88.

Dupuy, Judy. "Choreography for Television." <u>Dance - Screen & Stage</u>: June 1947, v.xxi, n.6

Steele, Thomas. "Remembering Harold Lang." <u>Chico News & Review</u>:

OTHER MATERIALS:

VHS:

Hanya: Portrait of a Pioneer (1988) interview with Harold Lang on staging of *Kiss Me, Kate*

Shower of Stars *(copy from kinescope)* starring Ethel Merman, 1952

Interviews & Thesis:

"Fancy Free and On The Town"

Masters thesis by Danni Bayles; California State University, Chico (1980)

"Footnotes"

an interview with Harold Lang by Helene Vandenplas; CSU, Chico (1984)

"Reminiscences II of Ballet Russes Dancers"

Ballet Russes; Celebration of the Legacy. New Orleans (2000)

<u>Dec. 21, 1980</u>

Harold, reacting in typical fashion to the news of his 60th birthday.

(standing above: Tom Kinnee and author)

About the Author:

Danni Bayles-Yeager met Harold Lang in 1970 and continued as his student and friend until his death in 1985. She earned her BA (Drama/Dance) from California State University, Chico in 1974 and her Masters (Theatre) in 1980 with a thesis entitled *'Fancy Free' and 'On The Town'*, for which she owes Harold a large debt of gratitude.

She taught classes in dance and drama at schools in Northern California for many years -- most notably at Shasta College from 1978 to 1989 -- until taking a second Masters degree from UCLA (Library and Information Science) in 1998. She currently teaches computer technology for the disabled in San Bernardino, CA., where she lives with her husband, Matt (Storm Water Manger /San Bernardino Co. Flood Control), and their 5 dogs and 7 cats (at the time of writing, but by the time you read it, who knows?).

Harold Lang and Danni Bayles (Yeager) - 1985

"Harold was already quite ill when this photo was taken. Knowing how sick he looked he'd stopped letting us take pictures, but I was determined to have one last photo with him. With a friend's help I took him by surprise at a party, and he was horrified. The drawstring pants are a telltale sign of how the cancer was changing him; he never would have worn sweatpants in public, but now they were the only pants he could get on by himself.

He was as angry as he'd ever been with me that evening. I was contrite and apologized for disobeying, but I've never been sorry to have this picture."

To Danni
A Good friend.
Love, Harold
"Lang"

Dec. 21, 1980

ISBN 141207135-6